"This profound and elegantly written book defies ordinary categories and expectations. It is part spiritual travelogue, part historical narrative, part meditative reflection, and part prophetic witness. Brigid emerges as a bridge builder who synthesizes the sacred and the secular, the pagan past with the Christian future, physical health with spiritual well-being, local rituals with universal hopes, female power with patriarchal order, and the natural world with the transcendent dimension."

—Lee Barrett, PhD, Mary B. and Henry P. Stager Chair in Theology, Lancaster Theological Seminary, Lancaster, Pennsylvania

"A very well-written and accessible introduction to the figure of Brigid of Ireland and to the living memories still kept alive and thriving today, especially at the Brigid wells that proliferate in the Irish countryside."

—Mary Condren, ThD, author of *The Serpent and the Goddess: Women, Religion, and Power in Celtic Ireland*, and professor at Trinity College Dublin

"Journalist and author Nancy Fitzgerald takes the reader on a wondrous pilgrimage—a journey to meet the living tradition of St. Brigid of Ireland. We are met with a lively, living tradition of relationship, profound affection, and transformation. Grounded in history, enriched by stories, and centered in a deep desire for renewal, *Brigid's Mantle* is a delight to read. Highly recommended."

—Mary C. Earle, Episcopal priest and author of *Holy Companions: Spiritual Practices of the Celtic Saints*

"Scholarship about Brigid is burgeoning as people realize that she, along with and perhaps more than Patrick, defines Irish spirituality. The single claim that Brigid's idea of mercy, not sacrifice (as Dr. Condren has suggested), will be enough to fuel feminist faith for generations to come."

—Mary E. Hunt, PhD, Co-director, Women's Alliance for Theology, Ethics, and Ritual (WATER)

"Cloaked in rich detail, *Brigid's Mantle* journeys through the legacy and legend of St. Brigid, enlivening her divine spark and spirituality for today's world. Through impactful storytelling, historical framing, and an appreciation of Brigid's model of fiery, prophetic obedience, Fitzgerald's contribution to the unfolding story of St. Brigid is an essential read."

—Kate McElwee, Executive Director,
Women's Ordination Conference

"Like a most inspiring tour guide, Nancy Fitzgerald draws you into the world of Brigid, an often-neglected Irish saint of ages past whose remarkable adventures can help open the doors of imagination into what might be possible in your own life now. This is a book you will want to return to again and again."

—C.K. Robertson, PhD, canon to the Presiding Bishop of
The Episcopal Church and author of *Barnabas vs. Paul*

Brigid's Mantle

BRIGID'S MANTLE

Finding the
Fiery Saint of Kildare
at the Heart of
Celtic Spirituality

NANCY FITZGERALD

Paulist Press
New York / Mahwah, NJ

Unless otherwise noted, the Scripture quotations contained herein are from the New Revised Standard Edition Bible © 1989 by the Division of Christian Education of the National Council of Churches of Christ in the U.S.A. Used by permission. All rights reserved.

Cover images by Thoom / Shutterstock.com
Cover and book design by Lynn Else

Copyright © 2025 by Nancy Fitzgerald

All rights reserved. No part of this publication may be reproduced, stored in a retrieval system, or transmitted in any form or by any means, electronic, mechanical, photocopying, recording, scanning, or otherwise, without either the prior written permission of the Publisher, or authorization through payment of the appropriate per-copy fee to the Copyright Clearance Center, Inc., www.copyright.com. Requests to the Publisher for permission should be addressed to the Permissions Department, Paulist Press, permissions@paulistpress.com.

Library of Congress Cataloging-in-Publication Data
Names: Fitzgerald, Nancy, author.
Title: Brigid's mantle : finding the fiery saint of Kildare at the heart of Celtic spirituality / Nancy Fitzgerald.
Description: New York: Paulist Press, [2025] | Includes index. | Summary: "This book uses new research to understand women's roles in the early Irish church, led by Saint Brigid, to help women in the church today as we work together to deepen our faith"— Provided by publisher.
Identifiers: LCCN 2024036557 (print) | LCCN 2024036558 (ebook) | ISBN 9780809157198 (paperback) | ISBN 9780809188864 (ebook)
Subjects: LCSH: Brigid, of Ireland, Saint, approximately 453-approximately 524. | Christian women saints—Ireland—Biography. | Abbesses, Christian—Ireland—Biography.
Classification: LCC BR1720.B74 F58 2025 (print) | LCC BR1720.B74 (ebook) | DDC 270.2092 [B]—dc23/eng/20241206
LC record available at https://lccn.loc.gov/2024036557
LC ebook record available at https://lccn.loc.gov/2024036558

ISBN 978-0-8091-5719-8 (paperback)
ISBN 978-0-8091-8886-4 (ebook)

Published by Paulist Press
997 Macarthur Boulevard
Mahwah, NJ 07430
www.paulistpress.com

Printed and bound in the
United States of America

To my grandchildren
Eleanore Kathleen, Josephine Mae,
Martel Makoto, and Callum Emmett

May they live lives of happiness and purpose,
always wrapped in the joy of God's love, the care of
their family, and the comfort of Brigid's mantle.

CONTENTS

Foreword *by Katharine Jefferts Schori* xi
Acknowledgments.. xiii
Introduction: On the Path with Brigid xvii
Chapter 1: Brigid and Mary: Soul Sisters
    Brigid's Path Goes Underground.. 1
Chapter 2: Castlemagner, County Cork
    Something Old, Something New: Living into Brigid's
        Traditions 14
Chapter 3: Killare, County Westmeath
    Turning Back the Streams of War: Brigid the Peacemaker 31
Chapter 4: Liscannor, County Clare
    On the Path of Blessing and Change 41
Chapter 5: Cliffoney, County Sligo
    Wishing and Hoping: Imagining a New Path with Brigid 51
Chapter 6: Faughart, County Louth
    Ablaze with God's Love: Following the Light of Brigid..............60
Chapter 7: Kildare, County Kildare
    The City of Brigid: Finding Faith in Kildare 74
Notes.. 91
Index.. 105

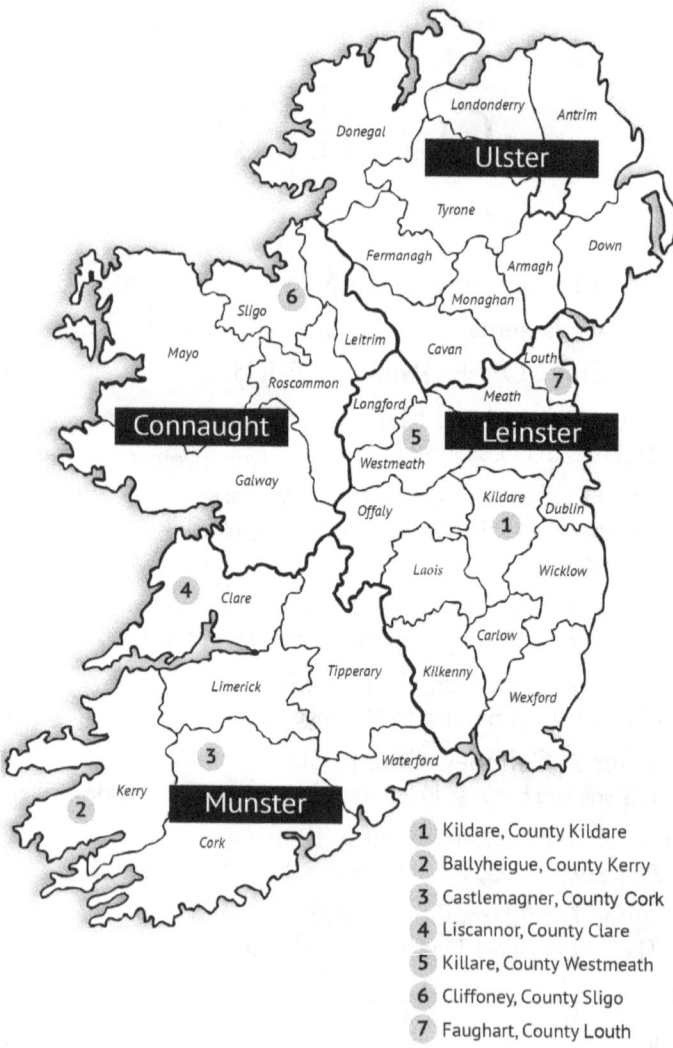

FOREWORD

Ms. Fitzgerald's thesis is urgently needed in an era when gifted and accomplished women are still derided, harassed, and excluded because of their gender. The world needs examples of female leadership that have thrived in and transformed their communities, even in the distant past; for it is the past, "tradition" in particular, that works to keep women's options small. Brigid and her spiritual sisters are a vital witness to God's expansive future. God continues to give us passionate and powerful women leaders—Miriam, Mary Magdalene, Catherine of Alexandria, Brigid of Ireland, Hilda of Whitby, Hildegard of Bingen, Bridget and Catherine of Sweden—and their lives and ministries are remembered and retold generation after generation. Each, in her own way, has insisted that God is at work in her life and those of her people.

The valuing of women's leadership in the church is particularly important at this season in Earth's history. The Irish influence on Christianity has deep import in the face of creation-destroying tendencies fostered in other strands of the tradition, and women's experience is essential to our shared ministry—caring for and serving all of God's wounded creation.

Brigid's Mantle

Women continue to lead today, even in highly patriarchal church traditions. Women serve as president-rectors of religious universities; administer corporate hospitals as well as local parishes; teach children, seminarians, and adults; and care for those on the margins, including legislatively. How can anyone dismiss the evangelical leadership of the women who first brought news of the resurrection? For that reason the Orthodox call Mary Magdalene "apostle to the apostles." Some ecclesiastical wit noted that if the Orthodox Church decides it wants to innovate, it looks for ancient examples of what seems novel today. We need the kind of creative and faithful ecclesiastical archaeology that Ms. Fitzgerald offers!

Katharine Jefferts Schori
Former Presiding Bishop
Episcopal Church

ACKNOWLEDGMENTS

I visited my first holy well outside the little town of Corofin, County Clare, under the guidance of local historian Pius Murray, who introduced me and my companions to the stark, simple beauty of the Burren and the power of St. Colman Mac Duagh's well. A couple of days later, on a visit to Brigid's Garden in County Galway, Jenny Beale taught me to weave a pile of reeds into the distinctive shape of a cross; that's when I fell in love with St. Brigid of Kildare. Colman and Brigid aren't much alike—Colman, after all, lived alone in a cave for seven years, while Brigid couldn't seem to get along without a constantly shifting cast of supporting characters. They lived on different sides of the country, too, and probably never met each other. But they were both powered by their love for God and their determination to spread the gospel throughout the island of Ireland. And they each had their own assortment of holy wells.

That's where my travels with Brigid and her holy wells began, in the "Wild West of Ireland," with Michael Waugh and a band of fellow pilgrims. But my journey took me back to Ireland many times, to visit holy wells dedicated to Brigid, the Mary of the Gael. For that journey, I have so many people to thank.

Brigid's Mantle

First, of course, my husband and hero, Gary Shiner, who (against his better judgment) drove an SUV for nine long days on the wrong side of the road, on the wrong side of the car, down narrow country lanes and along terrifying stretches of highway in search of some of Brigid's most remote wells. For his unflinching (and often puzzled) support, I am forever grateful.

I'm grateful, too, to Melanie Ann Schaeffer, MFA, who came along on a two-week trek across Ireland, acting as driver, navigator, and friend. It was a wild ride, filled with friends old and new, and unexpected, unforgettable conversations, including one with a couple of members of the Garda Síochána in North Cork.

The list goes on. To my sons and daughters-in-law—Andy and Elizabeth, Brian and Alicia, Kevin and Lauren, and Patrick and Victoria—who politely listened to me drone on, and to my granddaughter Josephine, who drew splendid pictures of Brigid with her colored markers.

To Anne Thayer, Lee Barrett, and Greg Cary, my professors and mentors at Lancaster Theological Seminary, whose friendship and guidance gave me the courage to begin (and continue) the journey. To the amazing Shaelagh Martin, seminary librarian, who responded with grace (and remarkable speed) to all my requests, turning up hundred-year-old journal articles and rare books at the drop of a hat.

To all those who read early drafts of my manuscript, including Bishop Katharine Jefferts Schori, Christine Valters Paintner, Chuck Robertson, and Mary Hunt. To Father Anthony Dill, who never failed to ask me how my writing was coming along and who slowed down my progress with a book about ultramontanism. (Seriously. Ultramontanism.)

To my fellow board members at the Women's Ordination

Acknowledgments

Conference, especially Kate McElwee, who, in quiet ways, let me know that this was a worthy project.

To Sister Rita Minehan and Geraldine Moore, of Solas Bhríde Centre in Kildare, who offered the warmest of welcomes, hot tea and fresh scones, and a comfortable place to stay (not to mention good conversation and amazing insight into Brigid then and now).

To my friend Jennifer Hanshaw Hackett, who offered helpful comments. To all my friends—you know who you are—who listened to me patiently for a very long time. (Sorry, I think I've been a bit obsessed.)

To my agent, Kathleen Davis Niendorff, for finding a home for this book; to Trace Murphy, Diane Vescovi, and Leah Arabia at Paulist; and to my friend and former colleague, Henry Carrigan, for his invaluable suggestions. To Amy Wagner, Brenda Klinger, and Angela DeAngelo for their expert technical and artistic assistance.

My thanks to Pius Murray of Corofin, County Clare, for introducing me to the holy wells of Ireland. To my friend James Truett of Lissycasey, County Clare, whose photographs are a joy and an inspiration. To Paula at the Cahir House in Tipperary, who introduced me to a wonderful book on Brigid. To Ruth Illington of Mullingar, County Westmeath, a walking encyclopedia of all things Brigid. To Dolores Whelan of Dundalk, County Louth, who waited patiently for me while I sat at the wrong roundabout outside town and who inspired me not only with stories of Brigid but with her own close and personal connection with the saint. To Margaret and Martin Byrne of Cliffoney, County Sligo, who led me across an overgrown field and brought me to the most remarkable, out-of-the-way well where Brigid's presence remains strong. To my friend Lily Moloney, for

Brigid's Mantle

an unexpected visit at the Bon Secours Hospital in Tralee, County Kerry, and a chat with her daughter Tracey in Vancouver. In Ireland, you never know who you'll run into (in person or on the phone).

To Mary McAleese, former president of the Republic of Ireland, whom I met at a synod event in Rome in October 2023. When I told her about my project, she looked me straight in the eye and said, "You must write that book." I did, and here it is, with my deepest gratitude to everyone who helped me along the way. It really does take a village.

March 25, 2024
Feast of the Annunciation

INTRODUCTION

On the Path with Brigid

> Now Brigid is the equivalent to Breo-shaighead, that is, "an arrow of fire"; and she is not inaptly so called, for she was as a fire lighting with the love of God, ever darting her petitions toward God.
>
> Noel Kissane, *Saint Brigid of Kildare*

Once upon a time, on the plains of Kildare, in the Irish province of Leinster, there was a nun named Brigid.[1] She was a woman of remarkable holiness, renowned for her care of the sick and the poor. Apparently well-connected to the divine, she cured a local king of a serious deformity: instead of human ears, he'd been cursed with the ears of an ass (problematic, then as now, in his line of work). In return for her kindness, the king promised to grant Brigid whatever she asked for. *Here's what I'd like*, she replied. *Give me all the land my cloak will cover*. The king thought he was getting off easy. As the sun was setting, Brigid and her sisters began to spread the cloak. And by the time the morning dew had fallen on the grassy fields, the cloak was draped across thousands of acres of the Curragh, which came to be known as "Brigid's pastures."[2]

That was the last time anyone underestimated Brigid. She used some of her land for her double monastery of monks and nuns. It became "a center of learning, pilgrimage, worship, and hospitality" until the sixteenth century, when Henry VIII suppressed all the monasteries in England and Ireland.[3]

The story of Brigid's Mantle may be folklore—a charming little tale about a harmless nun getting a couple of extra acres at the expense of a clueless king. But it shows something important about Brigid: she knew exactly what she was doing. Spreading her cloak was an act of subversion, turning the king's false generosity upside down and revealing the harmless little nun as someone to be reckoned with. She may have been a woman of remarkable holiness, but she was also a woman of implacable will. She had work to do—and a gospel to preach—and she put her rugged, persistent, can-do faith up against the power of the king, betting that God would come down on the side of the poor and the hungry at her door.

It's been a millennium and a half, and the story survives. It's a sign of the power of the people on the margins and a reminder to those who are on the brink of forgetting about them. Across Ireland, even today, Brigid's mantle is still being spread. On the eve of her feast day, February 1, people hang a cloth outside their door, knowing that the saint will bless it as she goes by. It is, after all, their *brat Bhríde*, a symbol of Brigid's cloak. Even today, remnants of her mantle are still being woven into the story of Irish life. In the tiny village of Gleann na gCreabhar in County Limerick, for example, the

Introduction

schoolteacher, Pádraig O Cadhla, told a young folklorist in the 1940s:

> It was commonly held in the district that if you put out a piece of cloth on St. Brigid's eve night and measured it, you would find it was one inch longer in the morning. This cloth was a great cure for a headache. The cloth had to be bandaged around the person's head suffering from headache.[4]

In that remote Irish village, Brigid was still at work, working her miracles. She's still at work today. (African-American womanist folklore might call this "making a way out of no way.") It's been more than a thousand years since St. Brigid traveled along the bog roads and through the forests and visited primitive villages to bring the gospel. But her influence still lingers, if you know where to look for it.

I've been looking for it at the ancient holy wells in rural Ireland—now dedicated to St. Brigid but with origins that go back through the mists of time, all the way to the pagans. Nobody's exactly sure, but there may be a thousand or so sacred springs in Ireland, and a few hundred of them belong to Brigid—more than those dedicated to any other saint. Each one can tell us something not only about this woman but also about the part that women played in the early days of Christianity in Ireland. Even more importantly, Brigid's holy wells can give us a hint of how women can change the church today.

Before Christianity arrived, those springs were holy places, where people gathered to worship, inaugurate their kings, and mark the passing of the seasons. As the Christian missionaries brought a new religion to Ireland, some things changed forever. And some things stayed exactly the same.

Let's begin at the beginning. Who exactly was Brigid, anyway?

BRIGID AND THE OLD RELIGION

A near-contemporary of Patrick, Brigid was born in about 453 CE, the daughter of a druid father and a mother who was enslaved. Baptized in milk, she was a link between the old and the new. Her childhood was marked with acts of generosity and kindness that set a path she'd follow for the rest of her life. She gave away treasures, from her father's golden sword to her mother's newly churned butter. Chances are, nobody in her family was surprised when she became a nun and dedicated her life to the new religion. After all, they'd noticed flames shooting from her head since infancy; they must have guessed that she was destined for something great. And she was: along with Patrick, she nurtured Christianity on her island outpost at the edge of the Atlantic.

But before Patrick and Brigid, there was an ancient pagan religious system already in place. It had created the Neolithic marvel of Brú na Bóinne, a complex that included Newgrange, a passage tomb built centuries before the Egyptian pyramids. When Patrick arrived sometime in the fifth century, impelled by a message he'd heard in a dream, he found a few hundred warrior kings who ruled little fiefdoms known as *tuatha*. And he found a society that offered special privileges to poets, both male and female.

Introduction

There was a complex Irish legal code, too. Known as Brehon law, it allowed women to choose their husbands and to divorce men who were abusive. They could travel on their own and, in a limited way, inherit and control their own property. Lisa Bitel, a medieval historian specializing in Ireland and England, writes in *Land of Women*:

> Women in Ireland were no goddess-queens, but neither were most of them prisoners or slaves. They were participants in the culture, members of their society, players in politics, and partners in the economy....Early medieval European societies assigned to women a limited set of roles to play, but women in Ireland, as elsewhere, colluded in creating and maintaining those roles, as well as subverting them.[5]

Sometimes, women even took on leadership positions: when members of the Irish professional classes had no sons, they trained their daughters to be physicians and judges.[6] Women even played roles in religious life, writes historian Christina Harrington in *Women in a Celtic Church*:

> They were recognized as "religious professionals" associated with druids....Women in a range of high-status professions were accorded a high level of autonomy and legal competence, and the list included some who performed druid-like activities: female miracle-workers, female war-mediators, female druids, and female poets (the *fili* were a profession derivative of druidry with

very high status and quasi-magical powers attributed to them).[7]

The religion the Irish practiced on the eve of Christianity was feminine, earth-based, and mother-centered. The Great Goddess who dwelled within the land, in the Otherworld, gave her name, Eire, to the entire island. The Irish also worshipped other deities, especially a pantheon of goddesses, including Brigid, the triple goddess of healing, whose power was symbolized by water, fire, and poetry. She and her sisters were found at holy wells and trees, the feminine sacred spaces of the divine and portals to the Otherworld, as Walter and Mary Brenneman write in *Crossing the Circle at the Holy Wells of Ireland*:

> The Otherworld is the source of power, fecundity, and wisdom, all of which must be thought of as different aspects of the same thing. It is an essentially feminine power and is identified with the earth....As a source of power, it establishes the power structures that are present on the surface world.[8]

Irish religion took its power from "the earth imaged as a goddess...power and creativity derive from the feminine images as goddess, earth/place, or woman/cow."[9] And the most beloved goddess was Brigid. But as the pagan world came into contact with Roman practices, as the native Irish "male warrior aristocracy"[10] strengthened, the woman-centered society of Ireland would eventually give way to something new. "The Triple Goddess would be replaced by the Trinity of Father, Son, and Holy Spirit, a trinity...no longer dependent upon

Introduction

the fertility of womanhood to fulfill its designs," says Mary Condren, Brigid scholar and professor at Trinity College, Dublin. "Women and the energies they represented were a fundamental threat to the new religious consciousness."[11]

BRIGID AND CHRISTIANITY

When the followers of Jesus began to arrive in Ireland, remnants of the matriarchy were still holding on, setting the stage for the creation of a distinct form of Christianity. It was, Condren says, a form in which symbols and images associated with the pagan goddess Brigid

> recur in the stories told of her as a Christian saint....Images of milk, fire, sun, serpents are common...while the themes of compassion, generosity, hospitality, spinning, weaving, smithwork, healing, and agriculture run throughout her religious *Lives*. Her sacred objects, her mantle, hair, and holy wells, were taken over into her Christian devotional forms.[12]

The most surprising thing about these devotions is that they have survived to the present day. Since the Reformation they've been frowned upon both by English invaders and Roman clerics, who tried to suppress the religion of the ordinary country folk who were still devoted to Brigid. For centuries, civil authorities worried about the excesses that might (and often did) follow the large and riotous assemblies at the holy places where Brigid was remembered.

Brigid's Mantle

Whatever the remarkable qualities of Brigid the pagan goddess, Brigid the Christian saint was a powerful woman in her own right. In some ways, the two are so closely woven together that it's hard to untangle them. After all, writes Condren, it's not easy to separate history from folklore. But, she insists, "there must have been some basis for the claims made about Brigid in the historical fifth-century period in Ireland."[13]

Most historians today agree that those claims were based on a real, honest-to-God human, who lived in Ireland in the late fifth and early sixth century CE. Most of what we know about her comes down across the generations through oral history that made its way into the genre of hagiography—the lives of the saints. Those are the stories that told the world about local Christian heroes. They were a combination of medieval tourist brochure extolling the saint's hometown and inspirational account of a holy Christian life. Embellished with flights of fancy and meant to be taken with a grain of salt, they weren't quite what we'd call history today. But, says Anne Thayer, professor of church history at Lancaster Theological Seminary, they're "an important historical source if read with considerable care. There is usually some 'there' there."[14] Within a hundred years of Brigid's death, writers had committed her story to paper—and readers and listeners found it entirely plausible. That's because the authors of saints' biographies are actually the communities who hold the saints' memories. "The author is not the expert," writes Thomas Heffernan, author of *Sacred Biography: Saints and Their Biographers in the Middle Ages*, "rather, the community is a collection of experts, and the narrative reflects this state of collective authority."[15]

For generations of communities in Ireland, Brigid is exactly

Introduction

what her story claims she is: a woman who preached the gospel, administered a diocese, celebrated the liturgy, absolved sins, and lived a life of prayer and service in the imitation of Christ. And that sounds pretty much like what a bishop does.

Case in point: Brigid's ordination, recounted in one of the earliest documents about her life, composed in the eighth century:

> The bishop, being intoxicated with the grace of God there, did not know what he was reciting from his book, for he consecrated Brigid with the orders of a bishop. "Only this virgin in the whole of Ireland will hold the episcopal ordination," said Bishop Mel. While she was being consecrated, a fiery column ascended from her head.[16]

REWRITING BRIGID

In later centuries, with the male hierarchy firmly in charge, Brigid's ordination would be called a fluke, performed by a drunken bishop reading from the wrong page of his prayer book. But Brigid's life shows her, time and again, clearly living out her episcopal orders—and passing her episcopal authority on to her successor abbesses at her monastery at Kildare. In *The Hidden History of Women's Ordination*, Gary Macy, theology professor at Santa Clara University, writes that Brigid

> was referred to as a bishop not out of courtesy or metaphorically. She was really ordained...and there is no question that the ordination took. As

Brigid's Mantle

> Bishop Mel realized, Brigid, once consecrated, *was* a bishop....A woman could be ordained and even be ordained as bishop.[17]

Her ordination was no accident. And it was no accident that it's been mostly forgotten. Starting in the twelfth century, the church did its best to wipe out the evidence—and blot out the memory—of women's roles in earlier times. But here and there, fragments of the story escaped the purge: in Brigid's *Lives*; in historical documents like the Irish annals; in scraps of ordination liturgies lost, then found; in dusty libraries. To her communities, she was portrayed, like the apostles on Pentecost, with flames flashing from her head. To those "collective authorities" on her life, Brigid was an equal to Patrick, the apostle of Ireland. She was a descendant of those first bishops the apostles anointed in the upper room by the flashing flames of the Spirit.

There are those, of course, who see things differently. After all, they point out, the ordination accounts only appear in some of the *Lives* of Brigid. But how come they disappeared in later years?

There are lots of possibilities. First, there was the ecclesiastical and political pandemonium of the sweeping church reform movements at the end of the first millennium and the beginning of the second. One of the big reform targets: the islands on the western fringes of Europe—Britian and Ireland. The churches there had skated by for centuries, doing their own thing until Pope Gregory and other Roman reformers decided to bring them into line. Aideen O'Leary writes in *The North American Journal of Celtic Studies*,

Introduction

There is much correspondence to demonstrate Rome and Canterbury's efforts to instruct Irish leaders, in particular, on what they saw as proper, specific teachings and practices. Pope Gregory VII wrote a general letter to a prominent Irish king in the mid-1070s, urging...wholesale change in marriage-laws and ecclesiastical succession, among other allegedly deviant practices; and he claimed that there were serious irregularities in the baptism of children and in episcopal consecration.[18]

Ireland, of course, had long been criticized for unorthodox marriage practices, and until the eleventh century, the Irish baptized their babies in milk instead of water. Plus, there were big problems with ordinations and the succession of bishops.[19] Snippets in saints' *Lives* and other sources hint at unusual powers of women in the Irish church, too.

But there was more. (History—especially church history—is always complicated.) Around the same time these reform movements were underway, Irish kings and clerics were jockeying for position within the Irish church. Patrick's camp, vying for the ecclesiastical leadership of the town of Armagh in the north, was butting heads with clergy in the southern province of Leinster, who were pushing for their own home team based in Kildare. Caught up in the battle, the monk Cogitosus extols the glories of the "city of Brigid" in his seventh-century *Life of St. Brigid the Virgin*. Later, *Lives* of Brigid took the competition even further; they portrayed Brigid as an honest-to-God ordained bishop[20]—"a tradition that came to be represented in her iconography: even today, in most images, she is holding what is generally identified as a bishop's crozier."[21]

Brigid's Mantle

Which came first: the icons or the ordination? We may never know. But it's not surprising that some scholars take Brigid's ordination accounts with a grain of salt. According to historian Noel Kissane,

> It's possible that the tradition was deliberately generated in the seventh or eighth century in the course of competition between the followers of St. Patrick and those of St. Brigid for recognition of their respective saint as national patron. It might well have been that fearing that Patrick's episcopacy would tip the balance in his favor, Brigid's supporters propagated the claim that she was also a bishop.[22]

By the synod of Kells/Mellifont in 1152, though, the matter was settled. The bishops rescinded the powers held for nearly a millennium by Brigid's successors, and the province of Leinster lost its bid for supremacy in the Irish church.[23] The story of Brigid's ordination disappeared from her later *Lives*.

Since then, Brigid's ordination has been in dispute, with compelling evidence on both sides. But whatever really happened at her fifth-century encounter with Bishop Mel, one thing's for sure: eventually, women were cut off from religious power. "The fact that women could not celebrate Mass or administer the sacraments made them permanently dependent on men for those services....Somehow [the church insisted] the 'energies' of women would pollute their most sacred ceremonies, weakening their power and destroying their efficacy."[24]

Introduction

No matter what the hierarchy declared, though, just ask the people in the Irish countryside. To them, Brigid is still a bishop. At holy wells and churches, schools and GAA clubs, she's still holding her crozier (and sometimes even wearing a mitre). In the interests of uniformity—and to prop up the patriarchy—the church may have suppressed Brigid's status as a bishop. But the Catholic reverence for tradition counts for a lot. Sometimes, after all, the people know better.

REDISCOVERING BRIGID TODAY

Despite a thousand years of suppression, Brigid is remembered still. Over the millennia, the church has done what it could to domesticate her, transforming her from a firebrand who outpreached Patrick, trained up a generation of missionaries, and rivaled Jesus himself by turning bathwater into beer for some thirsty lepers.[25] Though you'll find more Irish churches named for her than for Patrick, she's usually relegated to second place among the Irish saints, pictured in her habit: a quiet nun living a life of quiet holiness. But today, people continue to remember her as something more. And instead of finding her at church, they are finding her at her wells.

That's where I went looking. From her well in Kildare town, the site of her famous monastery, to Liscannor, on the wild west-of-Ireland coast, to Castlemagner, on a remote farm in County Cork, I not only found traces of Brigid but the experiences of people who draw energy and inspiration from her. Outside of Dundalk, County Louth, for instance,

Brigid's Mantle

Dolores Whelan told me that she finds Brigid calling her in ordinary moments:

> I'll be coming home from town, and I'm on the roundabout, and I get a message from herself, "Come up and see me!" We all go through days when we can't think straight. And I come up here to the well and I just say my prayers here. And I say, "Brigid, help me to clear my thoughts." And that's what I do, to clear my thinking. Because as we know, our thinking creates our world.[26]

For Dolores, who's lived for years in the countryside near Brigid's birthplace, traveling with the saint has been the journey of a lifetime. For me, the journey started a couple of years ago, when I visited the west of Ireland—that craggy, heartbreakingly beautiful, back-of beyond that the ancient Celts called a "thin place." There, they believed, the veil between heaven and earth disappears and unexpected traces of the past are all around you. On a gray, misty morning in County Clare, my companions and I walked the Burren, in the path of Colman Mac Duagh, another sixth-century saint. Across that vast expanse of rock and bramble, we reached Colman's holy place, a well that seemed to transform all of us in subtle, simple ways. What is it about sacred springs like this one, hiding in out-of-the-way spots? I was captivated by these mystical waters and the stories they told—and the stories they hinted at.

Soon afterward, I visited a garden devoted to Brigid, whose story still lingers in mythology and folk practices and at hundreds of holy wells. Brigid tugged at my imagination, drawing me to learn more about her and the springs that inform

Introduction

faith and spirituality in unexpected ways. I was smitten. On later trips, I made my way to more of Brigid's wells all across the countryside of Ireland. Like seekers before me, I was astonished by what I found, by "the very existence and use of holy wells in Ireland today" and by the "continuity of early Irish Celtic myth with current folklore and Christian ritual practices...a syncretism of Celtic and Christian symbolism."[27]

I spoke with dozens of people who find strength and inspiration from those places and from this woman. I spoke with the Brigidine sisters in Kildare, who continue her tradition of prayer, service, and hospitality. I met with historians and musicians and farmers and people in pubs. I met a grandmother in County Cork who gave me directions to a well along unmarked farm lanes and asked me to say a prayer to Brigid for her.

What *was* it about Brigid, I wondered, that helped to power the story of Christianity fifteen hundred years ago? What is it about Brigid that continues to empower women today? And how can she bring traveling mercies for us, especially now, as the entire church (a little worse for wear) "journeys together" along the path of Francis's worldwide synod? It seems more than a coincidence that the culmination of the synod and the celebration of Brigid 1500, marking a millennium and a half since Brigid's death, both took place in the year 2024.

SPREADING BRIGID'S MANTLE

Gently and quietly, Brigid's mantle is still spreading—not only across the fields of Kildare but across all of Ireland

and around the world, too. As we mark Brigid 1500, her influence continues.

I'm not a historian or a theologian or an anthropologist. I'm a journalist, and in this book I've taken Brigid as my guide and my patroness. She was a poet and a storyteller, after all, and I'm a storyteller too. I hope to use my skills to tell the tale of this woman and to tease out the lessons she can teach us. The church throughout the world, still riddled with scandal, still keeping women on the margins, is traveling a path together as we search for God. Now seems like a good time to look at Christianity from a new (and indeed very old) perspective. The story of Brigid, who helped lead a church that understood and practiced the faith in a thoroughly feminine way, can offer inspiration for us. Brigid's story can help us spread a mantle of hope and joy across an old and battered world.

In the chapters that follow, we'll make our way to some of her remote country wells, using "medieval texts that describe a dynamic, bold, and essentially libertarian figure, traveling widely through much of Ireland, friends with kings, bishops, and lepers, reckless in her generosity, almost relentless in her miracle-working.[28] We'll find her

- *At her well in Ballyduff, County Kerry*, down the road from the highly developed Marian well (complete with stage, seating, and parking lot), we'll see how the story of Brigid is still suppressed (and how the people still hold on to her anyway).
- *At her well in Castlemagner, County Cork*, in the middle of a farmer's field, we'll see Brigid the Christian saint paired with the ancient figure of the Sheila-na-gig, proclaiming the strength and power of women in the natural and the spiritual world.

Introduction

At her well in Killare, County Westmeath, we'll see a well dating back to megalithic times, a pagan site that's been thoroughly Christianized, with stations of the cross, rosaries, and an altar where Mass is celebrated. We'll take a look at the common roots that grow our Christian faith.

At her well in Liscannor, County Clare, on the edge of a country road near the ferry that crosses to the Gaelic-speaking Aran Islands, we'll see the on-the-ground faith of everyday people as they find ways to make their faith journeys in joyful and tragic circumstances.

At her well in Cliffoney, County Sligo, beside a pasture of grazing sheep, we'll find a Brigid who lived a life of sacrifice, making the ordinary holy through simple practices that continue today.

At her well in Faughart, County Louth, Brigid's birthplace, we'll see a woman born on the threshold, in the liminal space between paganism and Christianity, whose life offers a word of hope: there is a new way, a path we haven't tried before.

At her well in Tully, County Kildare, down the road from the site of her ancient monastery, we'll look at Brigid's vision of Christianity, as she holds on to the forms of Irish practice while Rome attempts to bring Ireland under its umbrella.

Following in Brigid's footsteps became my own synodal journey, a path I have traveled with countless women in generations past. It was a journey through the present, too—and a look into the future. Brigid has spread her mantle throughout Ireland. In unmarked nooks and crannies, her mantle of care has been blessed by the water of her holy wells and by the lives of women and men who have been inspired by her.

Visiting Brigid's wells has been a mystical experience. It's opened my eyes to new ways of seeing the One God who is unseeable; of knowing the unknowable presence of God in unexpected places; of connecting my faith with generations—millennia—of Christians who have been seeking God, too. It's been an experience of communion with the communion of saints.

At some of the wells, Brigid seems to be laying low. "It is difficult to find poor Brigid among the Marian images and Sacred Hearts," writes Lawrence Taylor in *Occasions of Faith*. "Then again, that is probably no more than what Brigid herself did to whatever goddesses preceded her."[29]

Throughout the world, people have been finding Brigid again. Through them, she seems to be singing out loud and clear. In County Sligo, musician Meg Byrne[30] sings *Gabhaim Molta Bhríde (I Praise Brigid)*, an old song that rings true today.

> I pay homage to Saint Brigid,
> Beloved in Ireland,
> Beloved in all countries,
> Let us all praise her.
>
> The bright torch of Leinster
> Shining throughout the country.
> The pride of Irish youth,
> The pride of our gentle women.

Introduction

The house of winter is very dark,
Cutting with its sharpness.
But on Saint Brigid's Day
Spring is near to Ireland.

May Brigid—the patroness of springtime and new beginnings—be near to our hearts as we seek a new path leading out of the "house of winter, cutting with its sharpness." May Brigid, "beloved in Ireland, beloved in all countries," cover us with her mantle as we walk together.

Chapter 1

BRIGID AND MARY: SOUL SISTERS

Brigid's Path Goes Underground

> And there are some say Brigid fostered the Holy Child, and kept an account of every drop of blood he lost through his lifetime, and anyway she was always going about with the Mother of God.
>
> Lady Augusta Gregory,
> *A Book of Saints and Wonders*[1]

In the countryside of County Kerry, on Ireland's Atlantic coast, Jesus is known simply as "the Virgin's son." And though the chronology seems impossible at best, Brigid is called Mary's midwife, the foster mother of the Lord, and Mary of the Gael. Intrigued by the implausible connections, I was on my way to Ballyheigue.

Brigid's Mantle

A village with a couple of shops, a post office, and a bookmaker's, plus half a dozen pubs, it sits on the edge of the Atlantic Ocean. On a drizzly afternoon in the offseason, the fishermen and the surfers were gone, and there were no signs pointing toward the holy wells I'd come to see. But when you can't find your way in Ireland, there's always a simple solution: call in at the pub. I stopped at Flahive's on Main Street.

Here's the thing about Kerry, and about Ballyheigue in particular: if you looked anywhere else on earth, you probably couldn't find kinder, friendlier, or more helpful people. The Kerrymen at Flahive's were stars. They served up dishes of shepherd's pie and pints of cider and sat down with me not only to give directions to the wells but to ask where I was from and why I'd come to their village. They'd lived in Ballyheigue all their lives, but they were happy to hear anything new they might learn from a foreign traveler. After all, writes author Bryan MacMahon, a Ballyheigue native: "Not all secrets can be known, and the roads, fields, shore, and ruins will always retain their aura of mystery, no matter how much is captured in words and images. That is as it should be, leaving space for more discoveries in the future."[2]

Armed with full stomachs and detailed directions to the Lady Well, I set off in search of mystery—and, maybe, of a new discovery. No sooner had I reached the Lady Well than one of the lads from the pub arrived in the car park just behind me, offering me the local guidebook. ("There's some good stuff in here," he said. "It might help.") (There was. It did. I discovered again how deep Kerry hospitality is.)

Brigid and Mary: Soul Sisters

TRANSFORMING BRIGID

Presiding over acres of carefully tended gardens, pavilions for prayer and contemplation, a rosary path, and the stations of the cross, there's a grotto with a life-size statue of Our Lady of Lourdes. In her white dress and pale blue sash, she's a familiar presence all over Ireland, from Dublin to Doolin, from city churches to this remote outpost just yards from the sea. Why, I wondered, was she such a favorite with the Irish people? And why was she here, in the west of Ireland? After all, her connections aren't to Ballyheigue but to a tiny village in the Pyrenees and a French peasant girl named Bernadette.

The simple answer: it's complicated. There were a couple of things going on, all of which seemed to converge unexpectedly in County Kerry.

First, there were the remarkable events happening in France in 1858. While gathering firewood, fourteen-year-old Bernadette Soubirous heard a mighty wind, saw a flash of light, and experienced the first of eighteen apparitions of a lady who seemed to be the Virgin Mary. Over the next five months, the lady told her to pray for sinners and to drink from a nearby stream. Finding only a trickle of water in a muddy patch of ground, Bernadette scratched at the dirt until there was enough water to cup into her hands; within days a clear spring, which still remains, had begun to well up. During her final visit, Bernadette later wrote, the lady, "with outstretched arms and eyes looking up to heaven, told me she was the Immaculate Conception."

Bernadette, an uneducated girl from an impoverished family, wouldn't have known what that meant. But the priests and bishops who heard about it did. After all, the pope had just proclaimed the doctrine of the Immaculate Conception, affirming that the mother of Jesus had been born without sin.[3] The story of the Virgin Mary's visits captured the imagination of Catholic Europe at exactly the right moment and inspired countless pilgrimages and a wave of Marian devotions.

Next, the story made its way across the sea to Ireland, where it fell on fertile ground. Irish devotion to Mary was undergoing a resurgence that had begun with the Anglo-Norman invasion, when the English, at the pope's urging, invaded Ireland to (among other things) impose tighter control on the wayward Irish church. One of their strategies? Rededicating wells sacred to local Irish saints to canonized Roman Catholic ones. "So, for example," writes religious anthropologist Celeste Ray, "wells that had been dedicated to St. Brigid were rededicated to Mary....Irish well dedications to the Virgin may not be much earlier than about the twelfth century."[4]

It was a trend that continued into the nineteenth and twentieth centuries, as clergy tried to reshape popular religion by encouraging visits to Marian shrines while suppressing folk liturgies at wells devoted to Brigid. "Sites associated with the universal church [like Mary]," writes Ray, "were promoted at the cost of saints of local tradition."[5]

For the most part, the Irish seemed to go along with the changes. But while they'd always loved Mary, they didn't love her quite as much as Brigid, the "Mary of the Gael" and midwife to the mother of Jesus. "The Mary of local folk stories," says anthropologist Lawrence J. Taylor, "is a famil-

Brigid and Mary: Soul Sisters

iar character: she walks around...often in the company of Brigid."[6] In Ireland, Brigid was the leading lady; Mary was her faithful sidekick. Instead of grand titles and elaborate liturgies, Marian devotion in Ireland was embedded in poetry, prayer, and everyday language: in Irish-speaking communities, the typical greeting is *"Dia duit* (God be with you) and its response, *Dia 's Muire duit* (God and Mary be with you)."[7]

Local bishops and priests had their own reasons for wanting to reorder everyday faith practices in the remote parishes of County Kerry. After all, the Great Famine and the Penal Laws had left Catholics leaderless for generations, with almost no religious instruction and little access to clergy or to the Mass. So it was little wonder that in the west of Ireland a unique, freewheeling style of Catholicism had developed. And it was no wonder that when conditions improved, the church was eager to rein it all back in. Historian Cara Delay explains:

> Because the struggling Church failed to influence many parishes directly, Catholicism developed based on local circumstance. Although the religion they practiced may not have been endorsed by Rome, pre-famine Irish...maintained a strong relationship with the supernatural. Often to the frustration of the Church hierarchy, parishioners rarely distinguished between official and popular, between technically Catholic and clearly alternative beliefs and practices. The religion of most women and men was a mixture of the two; Catholic ritual and vernacular practices continuously interacted and intertwined....It bore little resemblance to orthodoxy, but the local religion

of the early nineteenth century served a clear purpose and contained powerful meaning.[8]

Little by little, though, by the time of her apparitions in Lourdes, Mary was having a moment, thanks mostly to the efforts of the official church, which stressed Mary's obedience and meekness. It could never be said about Mary as it was of Brigid, "She acts without asking permission; whatever she sees, her hand takes."[9] But in country parishes, the Irish continued to meld Mary and Brigid—so the priests and bishops didn't get exactly the Mary they'd been hoping for.[10]

Next, over in Rome, nineteenth-century popes and princes were desperately clinging to the status quo as popular ideas like democracy, self-determination, and railroad travel were shaking up the medieval world of the Vatican. The papal states had shrunk to a narrow swath of land on the Italian peninsula, while Austria, France, and Spain were vying for a piece of the Vatican pie. The response? Circle the wagons, and keep everybody, everywhere on the same theological page: the perfect path to harmony, they seemed to think, in a chaotic world. It was a mindset that brought about a movement called ultramontanism, which emphasized uniformity and the authority of the pope across the entire worldwide church. The doctrine of papal infallibility, which stated that the pope could not err on matters of faith and morals, was defined in 1870, and grew out of the concept of ultramontanism.[11]

The downside? (There's always a downside.) Conformity is nice, particularly in a crazy, unpredictable world. But "the increasing standardization and ultramontanism of the Catholic church," writes historian Mary O'Connell, "would also assist in drying up the local verdant landscape…for a

Brigid and Mary: Soul Sisters

new globalized spiritual economy."[12] Good news for Mary. Bad news for Brigid.

Meanwhile, finally, detached from the theological debates in the Vatican, the Industrial Revolution 2.0 was in full swing, producing and shipping a dizzying array of church furnishings, from vestments to candles to altar rails. One of the biggest markets was Ireland, where the Catholic Emancipation Act of 1849 brought on a decades-long church-building boom. Statues were in high demand; images of the Crucifixion, the Sacred Heart, and Our Lady of Lourdes were at the top of the charts, while those of St Patrick and St. Brigid had fallen out of favor.[13] The reasons were ecclesiastical as well as commercial:

> The most important were modern methods of mass production and distribution, which led to a much greater availability of cheap pictures and statues, but also facilitated tight control over their iconography and style—thereby helping to prevent the introduction of heresies. As well as regulating the types of images that were venerated, the church was also concerned with regulating how they were venerated.[14]

By the nineteenth century, Mary was the church favorite, and the few Brigid statues that were churned out in Italy mostly arrived without her crozier or her miter. And if the people still insisted on visiting Brigid's wells, the clergy found a simple solution: change the name to Our Lady's well. After all, Brigid and Mary were already intertwined in the Irish imagination.

Add some lovely landscaping and a statue of Our Lady of Lourdes and voilà. Brigid *who*?

BRIGID GETS A MAKEOVER

It's hard to know for sure, but there's evidence that around this time the Lady Well in Ballyheigue, with its "sparkling clear" water, its golden trout, and its history of cures,[15] was leaving its Brigidine past behind. But even now, beneath Ballyheigue's life-sized cement statue of Mary, Brigid still lingers.

> Despite the high level of Marian sanctions, iconography, and ritual, there remains a quiet influence of Celtic symbolism that is built into the traditions of the well and coexists with the Christian material without apparent contradiction. For example, there is a legend of a sacred trout that lives in the well. Further, the trout is linked to another spiritual symbol of Celtic power, the percolation of the water of the well. It is said by local pilgrims that if the water of the well percolates, the trout is present. We know from Irish mythology that both these phenomena are symbolic of the watery wisdom possessed by Brigid herself who was giver and possessor of this wisdom.... Although the cures may now be attributed to Mary's presence at the well, it is likely that cures were attained before the coming of Mary.[16]

Brigid and Mary: Soul Sisters

By the 1930s, and again in the 1960s, when the Ballyheigue well area was redesigned by the local parish priests,[17] Mary was at the top of the charts, honored for her "feminine" attributes of meekness and quiet obedience. She was the polar opposite of Brigid herself who, as a west-of-Ireland woman told folklorist Augusta Gregory in 1906, "was always going about with the mother of God."[18]

Brigid's presence at the Lady Well seems to have faded long ago from the memory of Ballyheigue—none of the folks at the pub had any recollection of the well having previously been dedicated to the saint of Kildare. "Especially during the papally declared first Marian Year in 1954," writes Taylor in *Occasions of Faith*, "local communities built the grottos—usually replicas of Our Lady of Lourdes with or without Bernadette...obscuring or displacing, at least visually, the local saint.[19]

But there are still those enticing clues that tie it to "its earlier roots in Brigid," write the Brennemans.[20] Meanwhile, though, if you're looking for Brigid, the locals will direct you a few miles down the road to the Ballyduff townland of Knoppoge.

BRIGID IN THE BACKYARD

It's remarkably easy to lose your way in the west of Ireland. Looking for the well in Ballyduff, I ended up in a farmyard where a little boy was kicking a soccer ball. "Where's St. Brigid's well?" I called out the window. He scooped up the ball and shrugged. "I don't know," he replied. "But I'll ask my Nan."

In no time at all, Nan came hurrying out in her apron. Before she could dispense directions, though, she needed to know who I was and where I was from—and to assure me that I was "most welcome" in County Kerry. Then she pointed across the fields and into the distance. "See that lane over there, where the tractor is going?" I did, sort of. "Go past that," she advised, "and drive up to the next lane after it. Turn right—the well is just down the road." As I pulled out of the farmyard, Nan called out to me, "Say a prayer to Brigid for me." I promised that I would.

After a couple of wrong turns, I found her: the larger-than-life abbess in a brown robe, holding her crozier and her little wooden church. She stood atop a mound of stones in somebody's backyard, presiding in the company of an equally tall Mary (Our Lady of Lourdes, of course) and a giant crucifix: the holy trinity of rural Ireland.

Just across from the statues was the well—a spring, really, horseshoe-shaped and surrounded by large granite stones, sitting in the middle of a marshy field. Its official name is Tobar Eilis (or Tobar Leighis, depending on who you ask). That's Irish for well of healing or well of hope. But to the residents of Knoppoge, it's known simply as St. Brigid's well. The saint stopped here, it's believed, on her way to visit her friend Dahalin, a nun who lived just a few miles away.[21]

We don't know much about the well, except that it probably existed long before Brigid arrived. Local folklorist and author of *Holy Wells of County Cork*, Amanda Clarke points out some of its features:

> This does seem like an ancient well, originally right inside or very close to a ringfort which is still incorporated into the rounds. Three rounds

Brigid and Mary: Soul Sisters

seemed to be paid here, all clockwise, *deiseal*, which included the mound or remains of the ringfort. Inside the well, the percolation is vigorous and the golden trout is a very good signifier should you see it.[22]

Known for its cures of "mental worries as well as bodily ailments," this isolated well has been a place of devotion for a long time and people still visit it today.[23] Young Eileen Sullivan recorded this recollection from her grandmother, Mrs. Michael Sullivan, in the Irish Folk Collection of the 1930s:

> There is a well about a half a mile from my house and it is called "Tobar a leighis." It is situated a few hundred yards from the public road. This well is called after St. Brigid. A lot of people go there paying rounds, and some people are cured. People pay rounds at the well on Friday evening and more on Saturday. People go on Friday for the health and Saturday for the head. It is said that persons who are cured see a gold fish in the well. The people that pay rounds leave a medal or picture or a bead near it. This well is opened to the public. There is a mound of earth near the well and it is circular in shape. Round this the people walk when they are paying the round. They say three rosaries for every round.[24]

That "mound of earth near the well [that is] circular in shape," which Mrs. Sullivan describes to her granddaughter, is actually the remains of an Iron Age ringfort, converted now to a place of Christian pilgrimage.

Out here, miles from Ballyheigue's highly developed Lady Well, the countryside is peopled with long-ago saints you've probably never heard of, and this neighborhood of Kerry seems to have attracted more than its share. Besides Mary and Brigid, there were obscure monks and nuns who worked tirelessly without leaving behind a written record. But they did leave little breadcrumbs:

> Tucked away in hard-to-reach places, you'll find the remnants of their ancient churches and monasteries, their holy wells, and scraps of folklore that local people recite. Just down the road from Brigid's well in Ballyduff, for example, there's one remaining wall of an eighth-century monastery known as *Tempeall Dathleann*, the church of St. Dahlin. We know next to nothing about her, except that she warmly welcomed her friend St. Brigid and she turned away raiding Vikings by "firing a fist of earth at them, immediately striking them blind."[25]

Originally dedicated to her friend St. Brigid, St. Dahlin's well is still known for healing all varieties of eye affliction.

Here in rural County Kerry, those little breadcrumbs still attest to memories that go way, way back. The hierarchy from Rome and the bishops in Dublin may have tried to tamp down devotion to local saints like Brigid and Dahlin. The elaborate Lady Well in Ballyheigue may have erased a simpler well, replacing a spring, a tree, and some stones with a car park, a modern sound system, and lavishly landscaped gardens.

But in the end, the stories of those almost unknown saints linger where they lived and worked and prayed more than a thousand years ago. The people who are steeped in those stories may only know bits and pieces of them. But they know they're part of something important that happened in Ireland—and in their neighborhood—a long time ago. The path from Brigid to Mary was paved by an institution in faraway Europe. But here in Kerry, at this unassuming spring in Ballyduff, Brigid hasn't been forgotten. I splashed some water on myself and made the sign of the cross, and remembered to say a prayer to Brigid for the grandmother of that little boy in the farmyard.

ON THE PATH, WRAPPED IN BRIGID'S MANTLE

The change from Brigid to Mary, write the Brennemans, worked in much the same way as "television did in Appalachia; it...introduced certain universalizing symbols that broke the self-contained and decentralized circles" that harbored deep meaning for people living there.[26] Traveling along our own synodal path, it's easy to forget that our conversations, our experiences, and our understandings can enrich us, while they turn us upside down.

Think about ways that your faith journey—your synodal path—has changed and enriched you. How has it forced you to see people and things differently?

Chapter 2

CASTLEMAGNER, COUNTY CORK

Something Old, Something New: Living into Brigid's Traditions

> Water itself is fountain and source, transformer, healer, and regenerative force. Its symbolic power transcends all powers. Water that is contained, as in a well, lends a spiritual quality to certain places, and it is these places that have demanded attention from the very earliest human experience to the present.
>
> Walter and Mary Brenneman, *Crossing the Circle at the Holy Wells of Ireland*[1]

In the west of Ireland, there's a fine line between past and present, sacred and profane, heaven and earth: crumbling medieval castles sit in the middle of cow pastures; famine

Castlemagner, County Cork

pots, once used to cook meager meals for a desperate parish, serve as backyard planters; holy shrines are perched at the edge of bustling highways.

There are ancient holy places everywhere, each with a unique spiritual connection. But some of them, like St. Brigid's well in Castlemagner, County Cork, are way off the beaten track. Stories about the well are recorded in the Irish Folklore Collection, and grainy pictures of it appear in scholarly journals. But it's not in any guidebooks and it doesn't show up on Internet searches. As we scoured North Cork, it didn't seem to be tucked away in the memory of anyone we asked. Even the librarian in the nearby town of Kanturk hadn't heard of the holy well right under her nose. But she did have some advice: "Call in at Geoff's pub just outside town," she suggested, "somebody there will know."

Somebody did. Sitting in a dark corner of Geoff's Castle Bar, nursing a pint of Guinness, was a fellow named Brian. A man of few words, he nodded and sent us a mile or so along rutted lanes, past a cemetery, through a gate, beyond "the big yellow house," and right up to the front porch of the O'Donoghue farm. It was an unlikely spot for a shrine devoted to the patroness of Ireland.

When I rang the doorbell and introduced myself, Lawrence O'Donoghue, an elderly man in country tweeds, didn't seem surprised to see me. But he did want to know who I was and where I was from. "I'm American," I replied, "but my people are from Clare." That seemed to satisfy him. "Come in," he said, "and bring your friend." He sat us down, my friend Melanie and me, in his cluttered parlor and gave us an hour-long history lesson. Then he brought us outside into the farmyard, past the chicken coop and the washing line, and pointed us in the direction of the well. "Mind yourselves," he warned, "it's slippery."

It was. On this gray, misty afternoon, we made our way down a steep slope and across an overgrown field to a grove of trees and the stream that fed the waters of Brigid's well. Long ago, St. Brigid—or those who were devoted to her—had been here. Before that, her predecessor, the pagan goddess Brigid, may have been here, too. And now, a few millennia later, here we were, at the small stone-covered well. There was no image of the saint of Kildare. Instead, Brigid's well was marked with a primitive carving of Sheela-na-gig.

In remote corners of rural Ireland, to this day, you can find Sheela's unsettling image in the unlikeliest places. Carved in stone, she's a grimacing, grotesque woman, squatting in the ancient bearing-down posture of giving birth, a throwback to an earlier, pagan era. She stares out aggressively, displaying her genitals for all the world to see. You wouldn't expect to find her in a place of Christian worship—or at a holy well devoted to a Christian saint. Yet there she is. (Scratch an Irishman, they say, and you'll find a pagan just beneath the surface.)

It's not unusual for Sheela-na-gigs to adorn churches and cemeteries. There's even one in St. Brigid's Cathedral in Kildare. But that doesn't mean the clergy are happy about it. Bishops and priests have tried for centuries to get rid of her, with little success. Even Cromwell and his armies were no match for Sheela's power. When she was threatened by ecclesiastical edicts or foreign invaders, the country people hid her—some of her images are still turning up today, unearthed by farmers in fields and bogs.

Castlemagner, County Cork

CHRISTIANS AND PAGANS IN IRELAND

Christianity may have spread in Ireland without bloodshed, but the old religion lingered for longer than you'd think, especially in the countryside. You can't, after all, build a new religion on the ruins of an old one without some creative compromise, says Barbara Freitag, professor of intercultural studies at Dublin City University. "The greatest difficulty the church faced," she writes in *Sheela-na-Gigs: Unraveling an Enigma*, "was to win over the peasants," who on the whole seemed perfectly content with the status quo. Long after Christianity arrived, they held on tenaciously to the "rooted and vigorously alive customs practiced within intimate circles of the medieval village community...unwilling to slough off ancient practices, least of all those which concerned them most deeply, like sickness, fertility, and death."[2]

With a sprinkle of holy water, though—or a quick sign of the cross, or a brand-new name—pagan customs could simply be baptized. And so, writes Freitag,

> Pagan rituals were overlaid with Christian elements. Sanctuaries around springs, wells, trees, hilltops, and other religious foci were turned into holy centres of pilgrimage and healing, with Christian saints acting as guardians. Many Christian festivals were fixed as counterattractions on dates already associated with major pagan celebrations. Christian saints were modeled on older deities, and accounts of their lives were often an amalgam of myth and folklore.[3]

Some of those rituals, especially the ones connected to Brigid, have continued, almost unchanged, into the twenty-first century. That brings us back to Brigid's holy well in Castlemagner.

The Castlemagner well has been a sacred Christian site for way more than a millennium, with a reputation "for sanctity and for healing such that large crowds used to visit on St. Brigid's Day," writes Patrick Logan in *The Holy Wells of Ireland*.[4] And during the eighteenth-century "penal days," when Catholic worship was forbidden in Ireland, the well was the site where Mass was celebrated in secret.[5]

CUT FROM THE SAME CLOTH

It's simple to see a connection between Brigid the pagan goddess and Brigid the Christian saint. Both were linked to fertility and childbirth; to the intimate, ordinary, everyday lives of women. Over the centuries, St. Brigid has been the patroness of midwives, childbirth, and nursing mothers. In Irish Catholicism, she's come to be known as midwife to the mother of Jesus—an extraordinary feat of time travel. But Brigid, after all, *did* help to birth Jesus as she brought the gospel to Ireland. Mary Earle and Sylvia Maddox write in *Holy Companions: Spiritual Practices from the Celtic Saints*:

> To the Irish, Brigid abides in eternity; this seemingly fanciful belief reveals a perception that Brigid's way of caring and ministering were learned at the manger.... She is seen as the companion of the Holy Family, as Mary's trusted

Castlemagner, County Cork

friend and aid-woman, and as the kind and faithful nurse to the Christ child.[6]

Brigid the saint and Brigid the pagan goddess are different, but they're more alike than you'd think. Even Sheela is cut from the same cloth. The primitive, pagan figure in the act of giving birth might be a distant cousin to the pagan goddess of childbirth and the Christian woman known as Mary's midwife.

They're similar in other ways, too. Like the bold, brazen Sheela, Brigid looked the male luminaries of her day—Patrick, Brendan, all of them—right in the eye. She seems to have been perfectly comfortable asserting her authority: she outpreached Patrick, she ruled over a double monastery of monks and nuns, and she wielded power over storms and sunbeams and wild, vast seas. She embraced her own pagan roots, too (she was, after all, the daughter of a druid), while claiming spiritual authority right alongside her brothers in Christ. So maybe it's not too surprising, when you think about it, that Sheela's image is carved onto Brigid's well in Castlemagner.

Mary Condren, Brigid scholar and professor at the Centre for Gender and Women's Studies at Trinity College Dublin, writes in *The Serpent and the Goddess*:

> If Brigid made several transitions in her route through Irish history, that is not to say that her role as mother Goddess was ever completely eradicated. Indeed, her maternal imagery reappears throughout her career as a saint: Brigid is the mother of particular saints, and in the medieval church at Killinaboy her image, a sheela-na-gig, is carved on

> the top of the arch of the door, effectively allowing the congregation to enter the church through her womb."[7]

But Sheela isn't just a carving on a wall, a half-forgotten remnant of Ireland's ancient past. Late twentieth-century researchers discovered that in remote villages, there are living Sheela-na-gigs, too, old women who display their nakedness to dispel evil and repel attackers.[8]

Freitag also reports that as recently as the 1990s, a group of artists, writers, and photographers, on an Ireland-wide search for Sheelas, learned of a yearly tradition in which local farmers parade their cows past a Sheela to ensure their fertility.[9]

There's mythmaking going on, and storytelling, and bits and pieces of thousand-year-old traditions, all of them shrouded in mist. But it's clear that the three of them—Brigid the goddess, Brigid the saint, and Sheela-na-gig—are somehow twined together in Castlemagner.

Some of it, of course, is hazy. But this much is clear: Brigid's well in Castlemagner was a place that honored the goddess Brigid long before Christianity arrived in Ireland. And soon after it did, we know that the well became a Christian holy place, rededicated to the saint of Kildare. The stone house that shelters the well was built in the 1700s, but its carving of Sheela existed long before that. (It was taken from its original home in an eighth-century church half a mile away.[10]) In Ireland, there are layers upon layers, and surprises wherever you look. One thing's for sure: Brigid's force is strong here, in this corner of North Cork.

At some point, Brigid—or other Christians who

admired her—arrived in Castlemagner and sained the well that had been used for centuries as a place of pagan worship. According to the Castlemagner Historical Society,

> St Brigid's Well, like most Holy Wells in Ireland, traces its origins back to pre-Christian druidic religion and ritual, when wells were known as sacred wells. They were used by the Celtic druids for pagan rituals and ceremony. Celtic pagans believed water to be a source of life. It is therefore reasonable to assume that pagan worship at this well could stretch back four thousand years. The original month for doing rounds here was in February, which coincides with the druidic feast of Imbolc.[11]

February 1 is the day we celebrate St. Brigid of Kildare.

PEELING BACK THE LAYERS

In Brigid's time, there were no on-the-ground journalists jotting down her sermons, no film crews recording her countless acts of generosity. Most of what we know about her comes to us in a genre called hagiography—the lives of the saints. Within a hundred years of Brigid's death, writers—and readers and listeners—found the stories of her life to be entirely plausible. After all, Brigid lingered in folk memory too, so Christians hearing her stories would have found it easy to grant their collective imprimatur.

BRIGID'S PAGAN PAST

As deeply Christian a setting as the well may be to those who visit it now, the past still lingers in ways that would probably surprise devout Catholics today. Mary and Walter Brenneman, in *Crossing the Circle at the Holy Wells of Ireland*, written in the 1980s, describe some of the ways these crossovers happen even now:

> An Irish maiden, on the eve of her wedding, peers into a spring and sees a golden trout, which she describes as "a saint, perhaps." An arthritic old man carefully and painfully eases himself lengthwise under a large flagstone or table stone that is raised a few inches above the damp earth beside a spring. Women place egg-shaped stones picked up on the beach at a tiny spring.... Some combs, pins, a cane, and other personal items lay in a crypt surrounding a spring on a hill. A swastika-shaped St. Brigid's cross constructed of fresh green sweet grass floats on a cress-covered spiring. These are not accounts of ancient and historical incidents... rather of current living rituals occurring at the present time near certain Irish springs, now known as holy wells...in continuity from prehistoric times to the present.[12]

In Ireland, the Brennemans write, holy wells are "wonderful amalgams employing cross-cultural and transhistorical ritual practices. Healing incantations, kingship rites, druidic rounds, and Catholic rites are being performed at a single site either serially or simultaneously."[13]

Castlemagner, County Cork

The well at Castlemagner is a prime example of the past peeking through to the present. But if St. Brigid's well at Castlemagner, like the stories of her life, hint at her pagan past, why does it matter? What do her pagan roots tell us about the importance of Brigid then—and what she means to us now? Let's peel back those layers and see what we find. Let's look at some of the pagan practices she adapted for Christianity then—and see why they might be important to Christians even today.

The rounds. The stories of Brigid's lives report that she circumambulated the island of Ireland—a remarkable feat for a woman of her time and a nod to the pagan kings who preceded her, who walked the length and breadth of their kingdoms to establish their authority. (Today, bishops circumambulate their dioceses to visit the churches under their care; even presidents and prime ministers make the rounds of the countries they govern.)

That practice plays in popular devotion, too, through the ritual of "the rounds." Most holy wells have their own special day—known as a pattern (or "patron") day—when the feast of their saint is celebrated. St. Brigid's day, of course, falls on February 1. In years past, people would travel from miles around to remember the saint, reconnect with old friends, visit the market, and make the pattern, or rounds. They'd follow a prescribed ritual: they'd walk clockwise around the well and the surrounding area a set number of times while saying prayers—often reciting the rosary or making the stations of the cross.

It seems like a thoroughly Christian practice. But like so much related to Brigid, it comes with a pagan backstory. According to Brenneman, the rounds are a clear imitation of the practices surrounding the inauguration of pagan kings.[14]

Brigid's Mantle

> We see a continuity of this ritual circuiting at the holy wells today in the form of rounds or patterns, in which pilgrims at the well walk around it, always sunwise, as a central part of their devotion...the ritual of circumambulation. The idea of this symbolic ritual is that through the power of proximity and relationship, the one who circumambulates takes in the power of that which is circumambulated, and vice versa.[15]

But Brigid's circumambulation of Ireland served a different purpose: to bring the Christian faith to the people while establishing her authority as a leader in the early Irish church. She (or one of her devotees) likely blessed and circumambulated the well in Castlemagner. Today, those who visit her well continue to make their rounds, imitating their saint and carrying the gospel back into their ordinary lives. Today, those who make the rounds in Castlemagner are connecting with the power of the gospel and the power that Brigid brought to the land.

The Sheela. Most scholars think she's a fertility figure, imbued with sympathetic magic: just by touching her, it's believed, you can receive her power. It's no wonder that she was important in earlier centuries when childbirth was a harrowing experience and maternal and infant mortality rates were high. "In medieval times, you wanted a big vulva to ensure the child came out as quickly as possible, because a long, protracted birth could mean the death of the child and the mother," says Freitag. A major childbirth aid: making "the vulva flabby and big—such as putting butter in the vagina to help the baby slide out."[16]

Castlemagner, County Cork

That made Sheela, with her enormous vulva, the perfect fertility figure for the early medieval mother, for whom childbirth aids were primitive and mostly ineffective. But while modern obstetrics have made the process infinitely safer, even twenty-first-century mothers can be terrified by the prospect of giving birth. Infertility, too, remains a struggle today (nearly 20 percent of American couples are unable to conceive after trying for a year). So it's not surprising that many women turn to Sheela after seeking more conventional advice from their doctor.

Sacred stones. Brigid's well at Castlemagner is covered with a well house made entirely of local stone—and stones seem to play a big part in the devotions there. The reason, says Séamas Ó Catháin, professor emeritus of early Irish folklore at University College Dublin, may be that "the imagery of rocks and stones is strongly redolent of fertility and regenerative powers."[17]

On the day I visited Castlemagner, there were pebbles and small stones at the entrance to the well and loose stones that seemed to have been dropped into the water. Louise Nugent, an archaeologist with the National Museum of Ireland and author of *Journeys of Faith: Stories of Pilgrimage from Medieval Ireland*, writes that it's "customary for pilgrims to remove pebbles from the holy well as healing aids. They were believed to be especially beneficial for women during childbirth."[18] Clearly, stones were powerful to believers in Brigid's time. They remain powerful today.

The most remarkable stone at the Castlemagner well, of course, is the Sheela. Centuries of pilgrims have rubbed the carving, offering "worshipping caresses because the stone dust from her vulva is thought to have curative powers," writes Starr Good, professor of literature at Santa Monica College and author of *Sheela na Gig: The Dark Goddess of Sacred Power*.[19] If anything, she says, this practice is growing, notably at Castlemagner, where visitors, she reports,

> have scratched crosses on her torso, her forehead, her palms, her thighs—on every conceivable plane of her stone body, which gives the look of a severe tattooing. The custom is no relic of a superstitious past....Belief in her powers has only been growing, since she bears more crosses in later pictures.[20]

The sacred tree. The center of St. Brigid's ministry was a couple of hundred miles east of Castlemagner, on the other side of Ireland. She founded her monastery in Kildare, or "church of the oak." Clearly, sacred trees, borrowed from the religion of the pagans, were important to Christians, too.

Trees were part of the druid ceremony for the inauguration of a new pagan king. Known as a *bile* in Irish, the sacred tree was a source of feminine wisdom and a symbol of authority: it was, the Brennemans explain, "rooted in the past of the ancestors and linked to the sphere of the gods."[21]

Here in Castlemagner, the holy well is surrounded by a grove of trees, as well as by a single hawthorn that grows directly above the mound where the well is located. The mound itself was sacred to the pagans who worshipped here thousands of years ago—for them, it was a gateway to the Otherworld, the dwelling place of the gods. (They considered the land itself to be holy and named their island Eire, after Ériu, the goddess who ruled the Otherworld.)

Castlemagner, County Cork

Christians, of course, don't worship trees. But the saint of Cill Dara forms a bridge between pagan and Christian, even when it comes to trees. Here at her well in Castlemagner, Christians still tie bits of cloth called clooties to the sacred hawthorn above the sacred spring.

Trees, after all, aren't just for pagans. "They reveal a continued knowledge of pre-Christian religion in a post-conversion period context," writes Della Hooke in "Christianity and the 'Sacred Tree,'" in *Trees and Timer in the Anglo-Saxon World*. "The 'sacred tree,' could not be entirely eradicated by the Christian Church and much of its iconography and symbolism was absorbed and given a new meaning."[22]

For Christians, salvation history begins with the tree of life in Genesis and continues throughout the New Testament. The Gospels offer trees as examples of a holy, fruitful life; Peter preaches about the Christ who was hung on a tree (Acts 5:30 and 10:39); and in Revelation, "on either side of the river is the tree of life…and the leaves of the tree are for the healing of the nations" (Rev 22:2). Clearly, write the Brennemans, "both *bile* and cross are healers of a broken humanity, separated from the wholeness and goodness of the goddess or from God."

> When Celt and Christian met at the well, the sacred tree present there became a bridge over which the two could walk to join hands in a common symbolism, uniting in a bond that resulted in the Celtic Christian tradition. Some of the primary symbols that made this unity possible, that enabled the mutual acceptance through understanding of Celt and Christian, resided at

the holy well. The well, the center of Irish Celtic spiritual life, became the hidden ground of Celtic Christianity and remains today a primary source that joins together for the people of Ireland their church and their land.[23]

BUILDING BRIDGES AT CASTLEMAGNER

As Brigid made her way across Ireland, she transformed the faith of ordinary people into something new. She preached the gospel, founded monasteries, healed the sick, and fed the hungry: hers was a life of Christian service. And if she fit the mold of a pagan in many ways, she broke that mold, too. Her ministry, says Condren, reshaped "the religious consciousness of the Irish, forming a bridge between the old culture and that of Christianity. It was an uphill battle, though, as many of the old pre-Christian symbols and practices remained well into the twelfth century."[24] Stories played a big part in this, too. James Mackey, in the anthology *Celtic Spirituality*, writes:

> For the [Celtic] Apocrypha, in addition to increasing our knowledge of noncanonical sources, illustrate also, and much more importantly, that canonical Scripture texts were retold in a manner which simultaneously enculturated the Christian faith and thoroughly formed in scriptural terms the minds of the faithful. One thinks, for instance, of the insertion of the pan-Celtic goddess, Brigid, into the retelling of the infancy narratives.[25]

Castlemagner, County Cork

In Castlemagner, and throughout Ireland, Brigid was a bridge builder, connecting age-old yearnings and fears and joys with the loving care of the Christian God. The old symbols and the ancient practices remained, but on her travels, Brigid the time traveler, "companion of the Holy Family, as Mary's trusted friend and aid-woman, and as the kind and faithful nurse to the Christ child," imbued them with new meaning.[26]

ON THE PATH, WRAPPED IN BRIGID'S MANTLE

The story of Christianity wasn't written on a tabula rasa. Even in the days of the apostles, there were no clean slates—there were certainly none in Ireland. So right from the start, Christian missionaries were puzzled about how to treat the pagan religions that already existed before the gospel arrived. They got some guidance from Pope Gregory about how to handle pagan sanctuaries:

> Water should be blessed and sprinkled on these temples. Altars should be installed and relics should be put into them. If these sanctuaries are well built they must be turned away from the cult of idols to the worship of the true God. The people will see that their temples are not destroyed and they will gather together in the places to which they are accustomed. In this way they will be led to give up their errors from their hearts and acknowledge and adore the true God.[27]

Brigid's Mantle

As we journey along our own paths, how can the example of Brigid help us find new ways to understand our old beliefs and misunderstandings? How can we see people and events in a different light? How can we "bless and sprinkle" holy water on them to help us "adore the true God"?

Chapter 3

KILLARE, COUNTY WESTMEATH

Turning Back the Streams of War: Brigid the Peacemaker

> She it is that helpeth every one who is in straits and in danger. She it is that abateth the pestilences. She it is that quelleth the wave-voice and the wrath of the great sea....She is the Mary of the Gael.
>
> Vita Prima[1]

The island of Ireland is divided into four provinces. Starting at the top and moving sunwise, there's Ulster, Leinster, Munster, and Connaught. And at the very center stands the Hill of Uisneach, the "hearth in the middle." It was known as the navel of Ireland, "a meeting-place between earth and the Otherworld and the source of all creation."[2] Its location made it the ideal place for the center of "an ancient cult focused on fire and solar deities," where every May at the feast of Bealtaine, marking the beginning of summer, druids lit a ritual fire that could be seen throughout Ireland.[3]

When the Christians arrived, they built churches where druids and kings had built their monuments and roads. Patrick himself was there, it's said, and so were the Irish saints who preached the new religion, using the signs and symbols of the druids to teach the Irish about Christ.

Brigid was among those early Christian saints. Her name was Irish for "fiery arrow," a good description for a woman with the fierce determination to travel to this hill of fire. She left her native county to travel to every part of the island—remarkable for a woman of her time—bringing the gospel along with her. She brought her fire to the Hill of Uisneach, where she "took the veil from Bishop Macaille," professing her final vows as a nun.[4]

In the collective memory of Mullingar, the town closest to the Hill of Uisneach, stories of Brigid have stayed alive for millennia. She's still remembered as a peacemaker who could connect with just about anyone. In the 1930s, folklore collectors gathered this story from someone in Mullingar:

> St. Brigid labored hard here, founded the convent and received many postulants in it. It was here that the ceremony of receiving the veil was first performed and from there the many other houses of St. Brigid were founded....She was highly respected by the chieftains then residing in the district.[5]

Killare, County Westmeath

In the fifth and sixth centuries, Christians were newcomers finding their way among warrior chieftains and druids in an ancient pagan order. But Brigid was at home in both worlds. After all, she'd been born on the threshold, daughter of a druid and a Christian. She knew how to relate to kings and lepers, soldiers and dairymaids—and she seemed to be content wherever she landed. So what better place than this storied hill to begin her consecrated life, among that illustrious assortment of chieftains, druids, and saints? At the crest of the hill, looking across each province of Ireland, she could find bridges between the pagan gods of the Otherworld and the God of Christianity. She was a woman who'd been born in the middle, and she took the middle way, connecting with everyone and always pointing them to the peace of Christ.

In her time, that wasn't always considered a good thing; better, it was thought, to stay in your own lane, among your family and your tribe. "In pre-Christian Ireland," explains Mullingar historian Ruth Illington, "authority came from the goddess of sovereignty. If kings were truthful and honest, everything was grand—the sun would shine, the harvest would be bountiful. But if the harvest failed, they were ritually killed at the crossroads, buried between townlands. So they were neither in one place nor another, with no access to the next life. That was the ultimate punishment—exile from your tribe. So the story of Brigid's birth on the threshold is saying that there's a new order here now, that people belong here. With Christianity, this is a land and a society to which everyone belongs."[6]

Brigid's fierce, fiery determination turned the old way of thinking upside down. She didn't care much for boundaries, and she seemed to fit in everywhere. It may have been here, among the Christian missionaries and the provincial warriors, that she honed her skills as a negotiator and peacemaker. After all, she ran into more than her share of conflict in this neck of the woods: She appeases a king enraged at a servant for the crime of breaking his favorite cup.[7] She fights it out with Satan in the home of a wayward nun.[8] She settles a dispute between a priest and a woman over a child's paternity.[9] She converts a reluctant pagan to Christianity.[10] She heals a possessed man "who had gone round the borders."[11] She tames a horde of wild boars who were "unable to resist her words and her will but served her tamely and obediently."[12] She prevents nine men "of a diabolical cult who were greatly disturbed in mind" from committing the murders they'd been conspiring to do.[13] She intervenes in a labor crisis, settling a dispute between competing construction crews.[14]

"Life in Brigid's day was very precarious indeed," Illington points out. "There was constant, mostly small-level warfare. The *Cattle Raid of Cooley*, one of Ireland's great tales, is mythology, but there were real wars fought for the possession of cattle. Your wealth was measured in cattle."[15] And most of those battles seemed to center on which cows belonged to whom.

Against this background, mediation skills were key as Christianity spread. Avoiding conflict came to be seen as a virtue.

> There was no lack of domestic strife in Ireland in Brigid's time. Feuds between clans were commonplace. She is often depicted as a peacemaker who intervened in disputes between rival factions and brought healing and reconciliation. Folklorists

tell us that in some parts of Ireland a Brigid's cross was often used as a token of goodwill between neighbours, indicating a desire for peace and friendship after a local quarrel.

One of the best-known stories associated with St Brigid is that of her giving away her father's precious jewelled sword to a poor man so that he could barter it for food to feed his family. Thus, a sword, a weapon of war, was transformed into a life-giving instrument, turning a "sword into a ploughshare." This story offers an important lesson for today when millions of dollars are spent on weapons of war.[16]

In a still-thriving warrior society, Brigid lived a life that was oriented toward peace. This put her—and the abbesses who came after her—into the category of "the woman who turns back the streams of war.…[She] gets involved in military conflicts, mainly in their resolution and prevention."[17] She came to be renowned for keeping the peace: she and her successor abbesses were asked to mediate disputes and even "had the power to pardon a criminal if they met him by accident on his way to execution, they would be entrusted with the 'safe passage' of certain prisoners."[18]

PEACE LIKE A RIVER

For Brigid, peace went beyond avoiding battles and defeating enemies. She lived a peaceful life in quieter, more mundane ways, too, as she cared for the ordinary needs of Christ, who presented himself to her, again and again, in the form of the poor. Basic needs, then and now, in County Westmeath and everywhere else, included water and shelter. So it's no surprise that soon after she took the veil, Brigid found a source of water for those in her care.

> The people granted her a place called Ached hí in Saltus Avis. While staying there for a short while, she managed to persuade three pilgrims to remain there and donated the place to them. She performed three miracles there, namely the flowing of the spring in the dry land, the meat turning into bread, and the healing of the hand of one of the three men.[19]

Voilà! Through Brigid's generosity, three of God's people had restored health, a place to call home, and a supply of fresh water. And for millennia to come, Brigid's followers in Westmeath have had a holy well in her name at the foot of the fiery Hill of Uisneach. They'd expect nothing less. "Ireland from time immemorial has been celebrated for its Holy Wells and Healing Fountains," an older resident of Mullingar told the young folk collector who listened to his story in January 1938. "There are some Wells in our own Parish…St Bridget's Well, which is very famous, is situated in Killare on the main road between Athlone and Mullingar."[20]

You'd expect nothing less alongside a hill that's reputed to be the source of all twelve major rivers of Ireland. We made our way on a sunny April morning to Brigid's well, parking along the side of that Athlone-to-Mullingar road, just past the Uisneach Inn and across from the inauguration stone of the kings of Uisneach. A short walk along a grassy path brought us to a small rusty gate topped by an

Killare, County Westmeath

arch bearing St. Brigid's name in metalwork (fitting, since Brigid is, among other things, the patroness of smithcraft). Inside, there's a big green field surrounded by a fence, and beyond that a working farm. Everywhere there's birdsong and—though we weren't far from the road—a sense of quiet and peace.

 Ahead of us was the well, connected to a stream that flowed out beyond the fence and into the farm. Could it be the stream that Brigid herself miraculously brought to life for those wandering pilgrims? Local people have believed for a long time that it is. In any case, it's very, very old, perhaps—as many Irish holy wells are—dating back to pre-Christian times. It's just as likely to be a pagan well that Brigid blessed, or that her followers blessed in her name. Whatever its origins, to the people of Killare parish, the well belongs to Brigid herself.

 It's a small, oval-shaped pond, bordered with moss-covered boulders. The water, a couple of feet deep, looks clear and clean, bubbling and flowing smoothly over the rocks and pebbles at the bottom. Along one side, there's a grotto, likely built around the same time the statue of Brigid was donated by a local woman in 1929. From a couple of flat stones across the water, pilgrims can reach the image of the saint and leave their gifts in front of it. There are rosary beads and flowers, a crèche, an assortment of holy cards, and a plastic statue of the twentieth-century Italian saint, Padre Pio. But above all these offerings, St. Brigid, abbess of Kildare and cofounder of Christianity in Ireland, is the main event: she stands there serenely, holding her little wooden church and her flaming lamp, reminding visitors that she's connected to fire and that she's the founder of a great and important church. (She's clothed, though, in pale Marian blue,

Brigid's Mantle

instead of the drab brown robe of the abbess of Kildare—another example of the syncretism between Brigid and Mary.) Across the field are the remains of an ancient oratory, believed to have been built by Brigid or one of her followers.

A gravel path winds around the well, intersected at points with stones engraved with Roman numerals; these mark the stations of the cross, part of the "rounds" that visitors pay when they come here to Brigid's little domain. And next to the water, of course, is the *bile*, the sacred tree, its bits of cloth a sign of the prayers of Brigid's followers today. Killare parishioners in the 1930s (and many today) still venerate Brigid at her holy well. Writes one contributor to the Folklore Collection:

> It is a place of pilgrimage on Good Friday by people of the locality. The pilgrims do Stations of the Cross around the well. Three requests are asked of St Brigid, one of which is hoped to be granted. The supplicant puts a coin under the statue of St Brigid to show respect for the saint. People go at different times during the year when they need favors but Good Friday is the day of special pilgrimage. Requests asked of St Brigid at the well have been granted.[21]

This patch of land, with its well and stream, has belonged to Brigid for more than a thousand years. But before that, it likely belonged to the followers of the old religion, who probably worshipped here too, in the shadow of the sacred Hill of Uisneach. It has all the signs, after all: its percolating water with the occasional visiting fish and its proximity to an ancient druid monument. For those long-ago people, says Illington, the well was "a way of touching the world of the goddess. There may have been deities within the well, or communication with the goddess, and the idea of healing of powers."[22]

But all that changed when Brigid showed up. Historian Lisa Bitel writes that Brigid

> demonstrated her special ability to convert landscapes from wild to safe, hostile to habitable, ill-defined to specifically Christian....[Her journey was] a sacralizing progress through an imperfect natural world full of pain, illness, hunger, and injustice.[23]

Today, at the Killare well, Brigid has left her mark. The water is clear and bubbling and the trout shows up now and then; these grounds are a quiet and peaceful place to contemplate the middle way, the way of Christ. The well is still a place of peace.

ON THE PATH, WRAPPED IN BRIGID'S MANTLE

Peace, as Brigid demonstrated, isn't an abstract concept but a way of life, a series of small acts and decisions. Writes Sister Rita Minehan in *Rekindling the Flame: A Pilgrimage in the Footsteps of Brigid of Kildare:*

> Her life and her simple gestures remind us that the raw materials for peace-making are all around

us, in our hearts and in our relationships with others. [Her story] calls us to reflect on how we contribute to violence; it challenges us to be at peace within ourselves, allowing us to be peacemakers in our world.[24]

Brigid lived in a world riddled with conflict. But again and again she searches for a peaceful solution—from giving away her father's sword to solving family disagreements to mediating labor disputes. Our world is riddled with even more conflict: small-scale wars (and the ever-present threat of nuclear war), the proliferation of guns, and bitter political divides.

The working document of Pope Francis's Synod on Synodality (2023) called for a synodal church that "can offer a prophetic witness to a fragmented and polarised world, especially when its members are committed to walking together with others for the building of the common good.... This requires us to be agents of reconciliation and artisans of peace."[25]

As we walk with Brigid, how can her life inspire us to be "artisans of peace," to find a middle way in our conflict-ridden world, in our communities, and in our families?

Chapter 4

LISCANNOR, COUNTY CLARE

On the Path of Blessing and Change

>May Brigid guide us past crowds of devils,
>May she break before us the attack of every plague.
>May she destroy within us the taxes of our flesh.
>
>Ultán's Hymn[1]

Every year on August 15, my family went to the beach. A no-brainer: it's hot in the middle of August, and on the south shore of Long Island we were a stone's throw from the Atlantic Ocean.

But for an Irish Catholic family, the date was important. It was the Feast of the Assumption, a holy day honoring Mary,

Brigid's Mantle

queen of heaven. So the routine was simple, and it never varied: first you went to Mass and then you went swimming. If you immerse yourself in the ocean or a river or a lake on that day—any body of water, even a swimming pool, would do—you'll be cured of anything that ails you. "On Assumption Day," my dad explained, "there's a blessing in the waters."

We were strapping, healthy children without any ailments, but we were glad for a day at the beach, blessing or no blessing. I remembered those summer outings years later when I visited St. Brigid's well in Liscannor, a few miles from my great-grandfather's village in County Clare.

To this day, people from Newmarket-on-Fergus still make the pilgrimage to Liscannor on Assumption Day, bless themselves with water from the holy well, and swim in the cold Atlantic just down the road in Lahinch. When my great-grandfather, Thomas Fitzgerald, came across the sea to America, he may have brought the tradition with him. Maybe that's how it was handed down, through the generations, to me. And maybe that's why visiting Brigid's well at Liscannor was such a powerful experience.

It's a windswept, sea-swept place. You can catch a glimpse of it from the road, halfway between the Cliffs of Moher and the ferry port at Doolin that takes you over to the Aran Islands. But you can't really feel it until you walk past the glass-enclosed statue of Brigid—holding her crozier, her miter, and her little wooden church—and enter a dark, dank passageway that leads you back inside to the well.

The well is ancient and holy; it was ancient and holy even before Christians arrived in Ireland. Under a grassy mound, eons ago, it was known as the dwelling place of the goddess that early Irish people worshipped. It was the womb that nurtured the spring at its center and connected people with the Otherworld, deep beneath the earth. And in August, they celebrated the feast of their god Lughnasa, as they harvested the first fruits of the summer's growing season.

There were other mounds like these, with springs and groves of sacred trees nearby, where local kings were inaugurated. They followed same ritual: they circumambulated the well, sunwise, then drank from the sacred waters, symbolically uniting with the goddess and the earth, establishing themselves as part of the land.

It's not surprising that as Christianity took hold, people, little by little, went from venerating the goddess to venerating the Christian saints. Little by little, as the holy wells of Ireland were "sained," they were converted to Christian purposes and imbued with Christian meanings. Here in Liscannor, at this dark and sacred spring, their devotion transitioned from the pagan god Lughnasa to the Christian saint Brigid, the fiery woman who was patroness of midwives, milkmaids, sailors, poets, and blacksmiths. The tradition is that Brigid (and Patrick, too) went around the island saining the old pagan wells, bringing an end to the old way of worship and turning the holy waters over to the God of the Christians. The feast of the god-king Lughnasa on August 1 became the Feast of the Assumption, celebrating the Mother of God on August 15. The festivities retained many of the features of the earlier pagan holiday. But they held on lovingly to their Christian patroness, St. Brigid, too.

The well in Liscannor has belonged to St. Brigid for more than a thousand years. Pilgrims come here all year long, including of course on the Feast of St. Brigid on February 1. In older times, that day had been the pagan feast of

Brigid's Mantle

Imbolc, the start of spring and the day marking the birth of the lambs.

Brigid's well at Liscannor, like wells all over Ireland, write Walter Brenneman and Mary Brenneman in *Crossing the Circle at the Holy Wells of Ireland*, is a remarkable example of

> the syncretism of the rituals performed at the site of the wells. We find wonderful amalgams employing cross-cultural and transhistorical ritual practices. Healing incantations, kingship rites, druidic rounds, and Catholic rites are being performed at a single site either serially or simultaneously.... A priest [may say] Mass upon a Celtic flagstone under which pilgrims will later crawl for relief of back troubles. Rounds may be the stations of the cross or an *à soliel* pattern in imitation of the circuit of the pre-Christian king.[2]

When I visited Liscannor, Pius Murray, retired schoolteacher and local historian, told me that the well became especially popular during the time of the eighteenth-century penal laws, when Catholic religious practice was forbidden and priests were banished from the country. Instead, laypeople maintained their own Christian devotions, including the tradition of "patterns," those circular walks and prayers with strong pagan antecedents. The locals had already put their Christian "spin" on these pagan practices, praying the rosary or making the stations of the cross as they walked their rounds.

Those patterns continue today. Families visit the well on sunny Sunday afternoons. Alone or in small groups, in

Liscannor, County Clare

the usual gray drizzle, on any given day you'll find the faithful making their rounds, clutching their rosaries, and placing small stones at stations to mark their intentions and offer their prayers to St. Brigid.

When they finish their patterns, they enter the tomb-like passage that takes them inside the hill and back toward the sacred spring. Along the passage, they leave their "sanctions," little offerings of religious or personal items. There are small statues of St. Brigid, of course, and rosaries, and an assortment of handwoven Brigid crosses. But though Brigid's name is on the well, she shares the sanctions with other saints, too. Padre Pio is a popular one—there are holy cards and pictures in abundance of this twentieth-century Italian priest. The Sacred Heart is represented, and so is Our Lady of Lourdes, known for her nineteenth-century apparitions in France. But there are more personal items, too: Mass cards for recently deceased family members, baby bottles and teddy bears, and photographs of children lost or missing or dead. It's a heartbreaking collage of images; a peek into the suffering and pain that bring people here, to this dark and holy place, to seek the intercession of St. Brigid—or any saint who will listen to their prayers.

There's a lot of stuff here at the well. Pius tells us that the local parish priest, who nominally oversees the well from St. Brigid's church down the road in Ennistymon, "would like nothing better than to come in here and clear out all the holy memorabilia that people leave behind."[3]

And from time to time he—or someone else—does. But the sanctions reappear almost immediately, often placed, Pius tells us, by Travellers, the nomadic Irish ethnic group who practice a form of folk Catholicism. Maybe clergy, historians, and theologians would like to bring the well back to its pristine simplicity and its historical authenticity. But it's hard to know if that's really possible. It's hard to imagine that the ancient Celts who came here—and the early Christians who followed them—had the tidy, sparse, post–Vatican II sensibilities we may wish they had. They may have brought their own votive offerings, too.

There's a theological principle known as *lex orandi, lex credendi, lex vivendi*: the way you pray shapes the way you believe; the way you believe shapes the way you live.[4] Throughout Christian history, prayer has mostly come from the bottom up: the rosary, for instance, was a devotional aid to the scriptures for people who weren't able to read, and as it became more popular, it received the imprimatur—and the encouragement—of the official church.[5]

The stations of the cross, too, came from a popular devotion in which those who couldn't make a pilgrimage to the Holy Land to visit the places where Christ suffered and died could reenact that journey along garden paths and roadways. (It was only later that the church caught up with the practice.)[6]

It's a sign of the Roman hierarchy's reluctance to initiate change but eventually—sometimes kicking and screaming—blessing the change that bubbles up from below.

At Brigid's well in Liscannor, you can see the rule of *lex orandi, lex credendi* at work. The votives left for St. Brigid will break your heart: They tell vivid stories of fear and loss and desperation. They offer fervent prayers for divine intercession. They go directly to the root of the connection between God and humans and beg the eternal questions, Why is this happening? Can you do something about it? Is anyone listening to me?

In official church teaching, *lex orandi* may have more

Liscannor, County Clare

to do with the prayers of the Mass—their uniformity forms each of us throughout the world, it is said, into the image of Christ. That's important too, of course. But for the pilgrims who are begging for God's intervention, for Brigid's good word, the small heartbreaks that make up their lives take precedence. For them, these are the laws of prayer that lead to their laws of belief. For centuries—maybe longer—their families and their communities have come here to Brigid to seek her intercession. In the penal days, when Masses were forbidden, these devotions were the law of prayer that nourished their faith. This is still the law of prayer that guides the way they live their lives today.

It all makes sense when you think about Brigid herself. After all, she developed her own Christian traditions, often cobbled together from the official Roman practices as well as her own native Irish ways. And sometimes, we're pretty sure, she pretty much disregarded the official edicts of Rome.[7] At her well, you'll find other pagan holdovers, like the "clooties," bits of cloth tied to the sacred trees outside the well, now with a distinctly Christian flair: "As the saint passes by," explains Dolores Whelan of County Louth, "she sees the cloths and responds to their prayers."[8] And, of course, there are the waters of the well.

Deep within the hill at Liscannor is a dark, bubbling spring, surrounded by stones, lit by a few candles. You can kneel down here and say your prayers. You can scoop up some of the holy water and pour it into containers to take back home. You can use it to baptize your baby or anoint a sick loved one or sprinkle on a photograph of a person you love who isn't here anymore. You can bless yourself and your companions, too, giving one another strength for the journey. You can even splash a bit of it out of joy and thanksgiving—

life is filled with blessings, too, as well as sorrows. The well has always been a place to mark all these moments, reports folklorist Lady Augusta Gregory in her classic collection, *A Book of Saints and Wonders*:

> If Brigid belonged to the east, [a woman in County Clare told Lady Gregory in 1906] it is not in the west she is forgotten, and the people of the Burren and of Corcomruadh and Kinvara go every year to her blessed well that is near the sea, praying and remembering her. And in that well there is a little fish that is seen every seven years, and whoever sees that fish is cured of every disease. And there is a woman living yet that is poor and old and that saw that blessed fish.... "And within three days I had the sight of my eye again. It was surely St Brigid I saw that time; who else would it be?"[9]

These are the prayers of the people. This is the on-the-ground faith of ordinary humans, making their path along their ordinary—and sometimes troublesome—lives. It's a faith that's a lot like Brigid's, who took care of practical needs: Was there enough butter for the family? Enough beer for the bishops' visit? Enough bacon to feed the poor and hungry who came knocking at the door?

This is the power of ordinary people, too. Their *lex orandi*—their law of prayer—can shape their lives and the lives of their communities. Brigid's well at Liscannor offers historical precedent—and deep inspiration—for Catholics today who are seeking to initiate change from below. Brigid was a bishop then, so surely women can receive orders now.

Liscannor, County Clare

Surely they can become priests and deacons and even bishops.

At Brigid's well in Liscannor, it's easy to look at the official church's unwillingness to initiate change from the top. But eventually, it may come to bless the changes that bubble up from the grassroots, from the dark, sacred waters in Liscannor.

ON THE PATH, WRAPPED IN BRIGID'S MANTLE

The only constant, in Brigid's time and ours, is change. Successive generations, over the years, over the millennia, imbue holy places and holy practices with new meaning. "Some Irish turning away from the Church are turning toward folk liturgies," writes anthropologist Celeste Ray in her article "The Sacred and Body Politic at Ireland's Holy Wells."[10] They may not be saying Hail Mary's on their knees or attending Mass at their parish church. Instead, they may be creating new prayers and worship of their own, or engaging in moments of deep, personal contemplation. There are lots of ways, after all, to access the divine in these ancient holy places. Brigid scholar Mary Condren writes:

> Women have moved sideways from the Church because of the ongoing scandals, the control of women's bodies, and so on. I started off from that point of hopefulness about women's ordination but realized that nothing much would happen in my lifetime. Thankfully, moving sideways—

toward Brigid and her traditions—has offered rich alternatives.[11]

In the twenty-first century, people may not have abandoned Jesus, and they may not have entirely abandoned the faith of their childhood. But like their medieval ancestors who strung together their rosaries or walked the stations of the cross, they may be looking for new—and maybe better—ways to connect with the divine, right here, right now. They may be looking for a new lex vivendi—a new law of life.

How does Brigid's story inspire you to fill your faith with new vitality? What old ways might offer you deeper meaning today? Is your continuing spiritual path set in stone or is it open to surprising detours and changes that you might just find at the well? After all, says Celeste Ray, "Wellside rituals are thought affirmative of faith and Irish identity, and for whatever problem one brings to a well, the waters still offer a cure."[12]

Chapter 5

CLIFFONEY, COUNTY SLIGO

Wishing and Hoping: Imagining a New Path with Brigid

These were the wishes of Brigid:

"I would wish a great lake of ale for the King of Kings; I would wish the family of Heaven to be drinking it through life and time.

"I would wish the men of Heaven in my own house; I would wish vessels of peace to be giving to them.

"I would wish vessels full of alms to be giving away; I would wish ridges of mercy for peace-making.

"I would wish joy to be in their drinking; I would wish Jesus to be here among them.

Brigid's Mantle

"I would wish the three Marys of great name; I would wish the people of Heaven from every side."...

Whatever, now, Brigid would ask of the Lord, he would give it to her on the moment. And it is what her desire was, to satisfy the poor, to banish every hardship, and to save every sorrowful man.

Lady Augusta Gregory,
A Book of Saints and Wonders[1]

Ireland is a very old place, but in the 1930s, after centuries of oppression, decades of famine, a war of independence, and a bloody civil war, it was on the brink of becoming a brand-new country—as the ballad says, "a nation once again."

During their eight-hundred-year occupation, the British had tried their best to stamp out Irish culture, religion, and language, so by the early twentieth century the Irish language was becoming extinct and ancient folktales were being forgotten. Ireland was about to enter the modern world, but the old stories that would give meaning to the emerging nation were disappearing. So the Irish Folklore Commission began fanning out into back roads and tiny villages to collect stories and sagas, local legends and poems that might otherwise have been lost forever.

One day in November 1937, Patrick McHugh, the *múinteoir*—schoolteacher—in Cliffoney, County Sligo, sat down for a conversation, maybe over a pint, with a local fellow named Pat White, aged sixty. Pat told the schoolteacher about the Cliffoney Pattern that dated back to "the olden days." Every year on February 1, he said, people would flock into town to visit the well of St. Brigid, blessed, he said,

Cliffoney, County Sligo

by the saint herself when she visited more than a thousand years earlier. "After the rounds and prayers were said at the Well," he explained, "the people came into the village and remained there for the rest of the day." That's when the eating, drinking, and fighting began: "Before night," Pat recalled, "the village was covered in blood."[2]

The local clergy eventually put a stop to the excesses; devotions to St. Brigid gradually faded and so did some of the memories. The holy well is on private land now, unmarked from the roadside. So when I visited recently, my companions and I had to climb over a rough-hewn wall, make our way through pasture under the watchful eyes of the sheep, and tramp through acres of bramble to find the holy place.

Finally, there—in the overgrown brush—was Brigid, her crozier in one hand and her little wooden church of Cill Dara (Kildare) in the other. A plaque says the statue was erected in 1850. But beside it is a seventh-century stone slab, a couple of feet tall, inscribed with a Celtic cross and a deep carving of a swastika, the ancient symbol of Brigid the sun goddess and Brigid the Christian saint.

For more than a thousand years, pilgrims have been flocking here. Ignoring priestly prohibitions, scaling walls, they flock here still: on the day of my visit, the sacred tree beside the well was filled with bits of cloth tied to its branches by those who come to honor Brigid and seek her intercession. Somewhere, deep in the memory of Sligo, Brigid remains. According to Séamas Ó Catháin, "the old traditions of Brigid's festival survived and ultimately found a lifeline among the lower orders of society. The Irish country people...promoted the tradition with dignity, piety, and pride, assimilating it seamlessly into the deep Christian faith of Ireland, without allowing it to become totally submerged."[3]

BRIGID'S MANTLE

TONGUES OF FLAME

Just down the road, in the parish church, where the "Irish country people" of Cliffoney worship today, there's a tidy, stained-glass image of Brigid's cross. And every year, on February 1, children at Cliffoney's National School, just across the street, weave swastika-shaped crosses from reeds gathered at local wetlands as they learn the stories of the saint's miracles.

But they don't learn about the most remarkable miracle of all, performed not by Brigid herself but by an Irish bishop named Mel: in the sixth century, with Ireland in the midst of a transformation from paganism to Christianity and church leadership resting firmly in male hands, Brigid—at least one account of her life attests—was ordained a bishop.[4] She was recognized as a successor to the apostles of Christ and one of the most important leaders of the fledgling Irish church.

At the time, it might not have seemed as startling as it does now. After all, people would have been steeped in ancient Irish stories that cast women in leading roles.[5] In Brigid's time, the *filli*—the ancient poets and storytellers, who counted women among their numbers—would have told tales of Méabh, the fierce warrior-queen, and of Macha, daughter of an Ulster king, who seized her place in the royal succession against all male contenders. In Brigid's time, the druids, still practicing the old religion, would have kept alive the memories of goddesses who "permeated Ireland," a land where "the source of life was so integrally associated with women that it would seem to follow that the origins of life were female."[6]

Ireland wasn't converted to Christianity overnight, and even when most of the island was nominally Christian—a

Cliffoney, County Sligo

process that took centuries—the old ways lingered. So when new Irish Christians learned that Brigid had been ordained a bishop in the succession of the apostles, they might not have been surprised. When they heard that flashes of light rose from her head,[7] they might have made a crucial connection; those "fiery columns" may have sent one clear message to those listening to the *Bethu Brigte*, the *Irish Life of Brigid*: the apostles of Christ, anointed in the upper room by tongues of fire, were the first bishops, and Brigid, with tongues of fire flashing from her head, was a bishop too.

In Cliffoney today, Brigid, still alight with tongues of fire, still carrying her crozier, is still woven into the spirituality of those "country people." Just ask Meg Byrne, lifelong resident, musician, and local historian in the village where Brigid's memory lives on. Her memory goes back farther than Brigid the saint, she says—all the way back to Brigid the druid goddess. Look at Brigid's cross, she says.

> It's in the shape of a swastika, the sun traveling through the sky. Here, by the well, is where the ancient ritual—the pattern—would go. In the old religion, they'd move east to west, following the sun, and Christians continued to do that, too. I love the way paganism and Christianity dovetailed. Brigid was the last goddess of the old religion and the first saint of the new one.[9]

And though the well is on private land now, in a remote place in a remote county, people still find their way back here. There are still cloths tied to the trees and coins tossed into the well. And stories are still passed down in the village's oral history. There was a church and a monastery at this site, Meg says. Are there records of it? Maybe, maybe not, she responds. "I just know it from living here," she says. It's part of the folklore, the local history. "It was passed on to me. They reckon it was a monastery of Brigid near the well. She would have visited here for sure."

In Cliffoney, the memory of Brigid happens in people's lives as well as in their stories. Among the most honored sons of the village is Michael Flanagan, the parish priest whose generosity and kindness to the poor of Cliffoney rivals Brigid's own. A hundred years ago, he put himself on the line to demand that local residents be allowed to cut the turf they needed to warm their homes. Things didn't end well for Father Flanagan, but he was surely following in the footsteps of Brigid, who had spread her mantle of kindness and generosity for Cliffoney's poor in her time.[10]

For Meg, too, Brigid is a constant presence. "Brigid is very important to me personally because of the harp and the hands connection," she explains. "She visited a house where the people were so good to her. So as she left, she's said to have blessed the hands of the two children who lived there. Two harps magically appeared and the children were able to play them. I love that story." A decade or so ago, as she was learning to play the wire-strung harp, Meg found an old hymn attributed to St. Brigid. "It's called *Gabhaim Molta Bhríde*; it means 'Praises Heaped on Brigid.' It's a fantastic short hymn, quite melodic. When I first began playing it, people just didn't hear it—maybe their ears just weren't open to it at the time. But the other day I played it in a session and the other musicians immediately wanted to learn it. I took that as a sign that Brigid's voice is starting to be heard again. I was thrilled."

Cliffoney, County Sligo

Here is an English translation of this haunting hymn:

I give praise to Brigid, daughter of Ireland,
Daughter of all lands, let us praise her.
The bright torch of Leinster, shining across the country,
The leader of Ireland's youth, leader of gentle women.

The house of winter is dark, cutting with its sharpness,
But on Brigid's Day, spring in Ireland draws near to us.
I give praise to Brigid, daughter of Ireland,
Daughter of all lands, let us praise her.[11]

Here in Cliffoney, a couple of miles from the Atlantic Ocean, it's said that every night Brigid, "daughter of Ireland" and "bright torch of Leinster," would enter the deep, clear water of the well and stay there until morning. "She would spend the night weeping and praying," says Meg. "We're not going to go that far, of course, but I do think it was heartfelt—her humanity and her need to heal the world through her tears, through her sacrifice." Today we might call that cold-water immersion, and sea-swimmers like Meg understand. "I swim in the sea year-round," she says, "so I can see what she was at. It makes you think more clearly. It makes you stronger."

Brigid knew—and her followers today know, too—that transforming ordinary acts with holy intention makes those acts holy, too. That's what sacrifice is: it's not about deprivation but about taking the everyday stuff of life, giving it meaning, and filling it with holiness. The word, after all, comes to us directly from the Latin for "to make sacred." Brigid's example—in Cliffoney and wherever she went—is one of a simple life of holiness.

Is Brigid's moment finally here? Maybe. It couldn't come at a better time. Life in Brigid's day was not idyllic: there were petty kings and cattle raids and frequent shortages of food. And though Irish law granted rights to women—like the freedom to divorce their husbands or to own property— the island was no feminist paradise. "Irish women," writes Noel Kissane in *Saint Brigid of Kildare: Life, Legend and Cult*, "were governed by men at all stages of life."[12] For the most part, girls learned housekeeping skills and how to tend the animals, milk the cows, and churn the butter, but not much else. If we could time travel, we probably wouldn't want to go back to fifth-century Ireland.

ON THE PATH, WRAPPED IN BRIGID'S MANTLE

Life is easier now, in countless ways, but some things remain the same. In the twenty-first century church, for example, women are still governed by men. But Brigid, who transcended the strictures of her day, is an inspiration to the women of ours. She's a sign that something new can happen. "Brigid to me is the crossover between the druid pagan Ireland and the early Christian Ireland," says Meg. "And to think that happened so peacefully, without any bloodshed or warfare is a great symbol of what we could aspire to if we want to make changes. She made the transition from

Cliffoney, County Sligo

druid and paganism so gentle. I would love to see that happen again."[13]

For us, and for a twenty-first-century church in crisis, Brigid offers inspiration, courage, and a way forward. The voices of women, their ministry—and their ordinations—were important in early medieval Ireland, and they are crucial today.

How can Brigid help us find a path to a profoundly incarnational faith, deeply focused on the goodness of nature and God's immanent presence within it? How can the example of her faith, in which welcoming women to holy orders is natural and right, guide us today? How can Brigid and her sisters—and her modern-day daughters—help us reclaim the roles that baptism, and the ancient Christian tradition, call them to? How can Brigid's path of sacrifice—of making ordinary things holy—help us change the world?

What do you wish for? Can the example of Brigid's life show you a way to make it happen?

Chapter 6

FAUGHART, COUNTY LOUTH

Ablaze with God's Love: Following the Light of Brigid

> Burning with the flame of an inextinguishable faith, she turned to the Lord in prayer. The Lord immediately heard the voice and prayers of the virgin and, by the generosity of his divine power, he who is our help in adversity answered her faith in him.
>
> *The Life of St. Brigid the Virgin* by Cogitosus[1]

From the top of the Hill of Faughart, you can see the Bay of Dundalk to the east, and the Irish Sea, stretching across to England, beyond it. It's the site of the fourteenth-century battle between Edward Bruce, brother of Robert Bruce (of *Braveheart* fame), and the English forces marching

Faughart, County Louth

up from Dublin. For years, the brothers had been planning a "Celtic alliance" between Ireland and Scotland, and in 1316 Edward reached Faughart and declared himself king of Ireland. But on that same hill, just two years later, he met his end.

Faughart "is an ancient place filled with a history that is both gentle and fierce," writes historian Dolores Whelan. With its strategic location, she says, it's little wonder. "The *Sli Midhluachra*, one of the five ancient roads of Ireland, runs through the Hill of Faughart on its way from the Hill of Tara to the north coast of Ireland."[2] For kings and petty politicians and invading armies, it was an important location.

But some eight hundred years earlier, before the fiercest battle in Irish history, Faughart was the place where Brigid, the girl who grew up to negotiate peace treaties and "turn back the streams of war,"[3] was born and raised. Like her hometown, Brigid was a bundle of contradictions: a pagan goddess and a Christian saint, the daughter of a druid and a founder of the Irish church, a well-connected woman who spent a lifetime defending the poor.

The old religion was slowly fading and the new one was beginning to take root, and here on this grassy hill, writes Stanley Howard of the Royal Society of Antiquaries of Ireland,

> the setting sun casts his rays on those early labourers for Christianity, carrying their frugal fare, gathered and garnered with their own hands, to the home built on the spot where that poor little waif, destined to become one of the greatest saints in the calendar, first saw the light.[4]

Brigid's Mantle

All across Ireland, she's remembered to this day, especially here in County Louth, where she's a hometown hero. In this neck of the woods, she shows up time and again in the Irish Folklore Collection, gathered in the 1930s but tapping into memories that go back much farther. "St. Brigid was born in Faughart near Dundalk during the fifth century," fifty-three-year-old Pádraig O Ruadhain told his son Tomas, thirteen, a student who helped collect the old stories. "According to tradition," Pádraig added, "she had red hair."[5] Like a game of telephone, memories—especially those going back so far—may not be precise, but they're firmly held, with nuggets of truth and enticing details. (A mural depicting a larger-than-life, red-headed Brigid has pride of place in downtown Dundalk, just down the road from the Hill of Faughart.)

Out in the countryside, too, Brigid's memory is kept alive by the holy places named for her. But Faughart, her birthplace, is one of the most renowned. Recalls another 1930s storyteller: "There is a beautiful shrine at Faughart, Dundalk, called 'Saint Brigid's Stream,'" where pilgrims "leave many votive offerings behind them to testify the power of the prayers on their behalf." The storyteller tapped into the community's collective memory to recall that Brigid "was a woman not only of great holiness, but also of great zeal and energy in doing the work of God."[6] Down through the centuries, the ordinary people of Ireland remember their saint as a holy dynamo.

The sixth century was a long time ago, and if birth certificates and baptismal records existed back then, they're long gone. So for the facts on Brigid, we rely mostly on the stories. They may not be the impeccable, scientific sources that historians count on today. But digging down into them,

Faughart, County Louth

we find nuggets of truth about this remarkable woman, especially in her earliest days in this little town by the hill.

HOMETOWN HERO

At sunrise "on the eighth of the lunar month," writes the anonymous author of one of Brigid's oldest biographies, her mother, the slave of a druid, gave birth "in Fothart Murthemni" in County Louth.[7] It was an unusual arrival, and when seventh-century listeners heard about it, their ears perked up. After all, they'd been primed by the Gospel stories, especially the narratives about the birth of Jesus, which hinted—with angelic visits, foreign emissaries, and peculiar stars—that something unusual was about to happen. It was pretty much the same with Brigid. Her father Dubthach, along with his fellow druids, had already foretold great things for the yet-to-be-born baby. Before she arrived, the local wizard prophesied that the "bondmaid will bring forth a daughter, noble, revered, before the men of the earth. As sun shineth among stars, (so) will shine the maiden's deeds and merits."[8]

It didn't take long for the prophecies to come true. Immediately after her birth, Brigid was rushed to the local queen's dead newborn son, "and when Brigid's breath came to him, he swiftly arose out of death."[9]

Those who heard that story 1,500 years ago—and those who hear it today—had a pretty good idea of what it meant. The mighty Brigid, who would change Ireland forever, was neither here nor there: not quite pagan, just barely Christian. More than a nun, not quite a priest. Equal or even superior to Patrick, without the parades. Constrained, as a woman, by custom and tradition, but indifferent to the rules and determined to get the work of the gospel done in her own time and place. God clearly had plans for her.

All the signs pointed to it. It was clear from the rich symbolism and the colorful detail in Brigid's *Lives* that this child would grow into a woman whose life would point early Irish Christians straight to Jesus. Those who had heard the story of Jesus's birth—and those who had listened to the tales shared around campfires by the Irish poets and bards—knew that all the details were there for a reason. Though the stories may have stretched the facts, they got straight to the heart of the truth about Brigid, daughter of Faughart.

First, there was the milk. From the first pages of the *Vita Prima*, written early in the seventh century:

> When the bondmaid was going with a vessel of milk in her hand, and when she put one foot over the threshold of the house inside and the other foot outside, then did she bring forth the girl, to wit, Saint Brigid....The maid-servants washed the girl with the milk that was in her mother's hand.[10]

Listeners understood that her birth on the threshold declared that she was entering a new era, bringing Christ to an island that would leave the old religion behind. And they knew what it meant when they heard that the baby was washed in milk:

> The early Irish...believed that the soul passed to the infant through the milk of the breast. As

Faughart, County Louth

one of the *Lives of Brigit* claimed, "For it is so arranged by nature that muses always bestow the affection of their spirit on those to whom they provide the milk of their flesh." Throughout the ancient world it was assumed that breast milk transmitted to the infant the spiritual traits of the mother. Brigid was baptized in milk…and indeed, up to the twelfth century the Irish continued to baptize with milk.[11]

And then there was the fire, a recurring motif throughout Brigid's life: her parents took baby Brigid outside to look at the cows, and "the cow-dung that lay before the girl was seen ablaze. But when the wizard and the bondmaid stretched down their hands to it, the fire appeared not."[12]

And later, when Brigid's mother went outside, leaving the baby asleep in her crib, people for miles around saw the house burning in the distance. "A flame of fire was made of it from earth to heaven. But when they went to rescue the house, the fire appeared not, and this they said, that the girl was full of *the grace of* the Holy Spirit."[13]

It didn't take Brigid's father long to figure out what was going on:

> At midnight and while the druid was watching the stars, he saw a fiery column rising up from the house, from the very place where the slave and her daughter were. He woke his uncle, who saw it too and said that she was a holy girl. "That is true," he said, "if I were to tell you all the things she has done."[14]

Before she was even a toddler, it seems, Brigid was doing quite a lot, and the druids were clearly onto something. St. Brigid's stories are rich with symbolism that was meaningful to both pagan and Christian, but the author of the *Vita* made it plain that signs like fire had new meaning in a new world that would be drenched with the story of the gospel.

Finally, there was the white, red-eared cow, the only creature who could provide nourishment for the finicky baby Brigid. White, red-eared animals in Celtic tales are always magical creatures from the Otherworld.[15] And to Christians, they were a potent symbol of fertility.

So many details, all of them pointing readers (and listeners) to one obvious conclusion: Brigid would be a momentous figure in the early Irish church.

A CHILDHOOD ABLAZE WITH GOD'S LOVE

To early Irish Christians, of course, the fire that followed Brigid wherever she went had a meaning all its own. It told believers that the Holy Spirit was near—maybe in a sacred place or in moments of prayer or silence or in the life of a holy person. In Brigid, though, that fire was a raging inferno. It was plain as day to everyone in Faughart. With that fire, Brigid took the life of the Spirit to heart. It showed that she "lived by the Spirit" and was "guided by the Spirit," whose fruits are "love, joy, peace, patience, kindness, generosity, faithfulness, gentleness, and self-control" (Gal 5:22–23).

These stories were remembered well into the twentieth century, a millennium and a half after they were first

Faughart, County Louth

told. Here's one story that folklorist Lady Augusta Gregory collected in 1906:

> And it was angels that baptized her and that gave her the name of Brigid, that is a Fiery Arrow.... And all the food she used was the milk of a white red-eared cow that was set apart for her by a druid. And everything she put her hand to used to increase, and it was she wove the first piece of cloth in Ireland, and she put the white threads in the loom that have a power of healing in them to this day. She bettered the sheep and she satisfied the birds and she fed the poor.[16]

Everything she did, of course, was all about love; nobody in Faughart could miss that. And there was nothing Brigid loved better than an underdog (including actual dogs, whom she regularly fed straight from the family frying pan). She cured "an unpleasant leper" and sent him on his way with some of her father's best cows.[17] Determined "to obey God rather than his creatures," she gave away milk and butter to "the poor and to wayfarers," leaving her with nothing to show for her day's work. But no worries: the God she loved and served was forever coming to her rescue. Her butter-baskets may have been empty, but "burning with the flame of an inextinguishable faith, she turned to the Lord," who replenished her supply.[18] She never met a beggar she didn't love: she even gifted expensive priestly vestments "to Christ in the form of a poor person."[19]

Exaggeration? Maybe a little. But the stories are frequent enough—and similar enough—that they ring true, painting a picture of a woman filled with generosity and love. For Brigid, from a young age, the incarnation—God in human form—was more than a doctrine. It was a daily reality.

Young Brigid was also—and we can be grateful for this—a person who knew her own mind, who disregarded social norms when she was pretty sure God had other plans. When she turned away a suitor and spurned marriage, for example, her family was incensed.

> Her brothers were saddened at being deprived of the dowry....[They] laughed at her, and others were not pleased with her. [Her brother] said: "The beautiful eye in your head will be betrothed to a man whether you like it or not." Thereupon she immediately thrust her finger into her eye. "Here is that beautiful eye for you," said Brigid.... Dubthach said to her: "Take the veil then, my daughter, for this is your wish."[20]

She miraculously reattached her eye, of course, and devoted her life to Christ. She was fearless: happy to stand up to the patriarchy when it got in the way of God. Patriarchal authority meant little to her, and neither did the possessions and the trappings of the society she lived in. She seemed to like nothing better than giving away whatever she had whenever "Christ, in the form of a poor person" came knocking at her door.

It's no wonder her reputation lives on, especially in Faughart. Her "unusual birth on the threshold of a house, her connections with a prophesizing druid, her insistence on drinking only the milk of a red and white cow...established

Faughart, County Louth

Brigid as a native hero…born a hero, reared by a druid with magical powers and marked for greatness from birth."[21]

After centuries upon centuries, even after a bloody war was fought a stone's throw from her birthplace, the local people of Faughart remember her still, especially at her holy well on the Hill of Faughart. Dolores Whelan, writer, teacher of Celtic spirituality, and longtime resident of Faughart, led me there on a drizzly April morning.

FINDING BRIGID AT HER HOMETOWN WELL

"About three miles north of Dundalk," wrote folklorist Patrick Brennan in 1936, "there is a place called St Brigid's Stream. It stands along a bye road, and about two miles from the main road to Belfast. It was here that St Brigid was born….It is said that it was in the stream that she washed her clothes."[22]

Here in her hometown, memories of Brigid, passed down over the generations, are remarkably vivid and filled with creative detail. In this neck of the woods, her power is still strong. Dolores Whelan knows about Brigid's power firsthand.

> In the countryside, in places like Faughart, like Dundalk, like Kildare, like many places in the West of Ireland, Brigid is part of our spiritual path. You ask Brigid to mind it for you, to put a mantle around something, to protect it. And she is always there to help us with what we need. I

don't know when I discovered Brigid; I think she found me.[23]

Dolores helped me find Brigid on that rainy morning. Like my guide, I felt the powerful spiritual pull that the saint seems to exert even now. First, we passed the ancient graveyard whose tombstones are worn and hard to decipher. Then there are the remains of an early-medieval granite church said to have been built by Brigid herself, along with evidence of even older ringforts, possibly dating to the late Bronze Age. Archaeologists have discovered underground passageways and fragments of high Celtic crosses and the stone blocks that once held them. There are signs of the enclosures that may have formed the foundations of an early Christian monastic site.[24]

And there's the patch of grass known as Brigid's Bed, a horseshoe-shaped mound with pillars along its perimeter and, at its center, a black stone, which pilgrims call "Brigid's stone"; they believe it marks the spot where Brigid was born on the threshold of her father's house.[25]

The area has served for years as one of the "pattern stations," where believers still pause to say a decade of the rosary (or just lie down and commune with Brigid).[26] What purpose it may have served in the past is uncertain.

As we continue on our way, Dolores points out a rock known as Brigid's headstone. It's one of the stations where pilgrims stop as they complete their rounds—and a popular place to visit if you've got a headache or some problems on your mind. "I just come up here and I say my prayers," Dolores explains, "I say, 'Brigid, help me to clear my thoughts,' and that's what I do. And I clear my thinking, because as we know, our thinking creates our world."[27] An early twentieth-

Faughart, County Louth

century folklore collector from Dundalk insisted that this tradition goes back to Brigid's time:

> There is also another stone which can be seen at present—one day as she was praying she rested her head on a stone and when she lifted her head the mark of her head could be seen on the stone. Some people say that if you lay your head on this stone you will never have a headache.[28]

Little by little, as we walk on, the vegetation becomes denser: there are high grasses and wildflowers and rag trees and the one remaining wall of an early medieval church. There, ahead, is Brigid's well, a stone's throw from the threshold where tradition says that her mother gave birth, and close to the place where she plucked out her eye rather than accept the husband her father and brothers had chosen for her.[29]

Are all these stories true? Maybe. Maybe not. But this is a powerful place all the same. The well is a couple of meters below the ground that surrounds it and it's covered by a cone-shaped roof. Half a dozen or so rugged steps lead down to the water. The well is surrounded, as most Irish holy wells are, by rag trees, bits of cloth tied by pilgrims and day-trippers. Here in Faughart, there are hundreds of colorful rags, plus some rosary beads and statues and holy cards. Leaving behind these bits and pieces, a tradition that goes back to pagan times, was incorporated into Christian practice. "You put something on the tree beside the well," Dolores explains, "and as the saint passes, your ailment or your situation will be healed. The cloth falls off and your intention is granted." Here, next to this well, countless prayers have been offered by pilgrims who have brought their cares and their hopes to the holy woman from Faughart. Does it work? "I believe all prayers are answered," says Dolores. "I believe they heal in some way. They touch the root cause of whatever is hurting your body or your mind."[30]

For many, this well and the land around it is an occasion of faith, a place where people can access the holy. "In the Irish tradition, the wells are portals to the Otherworld," Dolores explains. Maybe that's why being there feels somehow mystical. The water looks clean and clear and pilgrims have tossed coins into it, a nod to another pagan custom. There's a small, dark stone-covered entry area at the entry to the well where Dolores and I pause as she covers us both with a rough-woven shawl that makes me think of Brigid's mantle. "Maybe we could say a prayer here," she suggests.

After saving some water into little bottles that we can bring back home, Dolores scoops up a little more and sprinkles it on each of us, showering us with Brigid's blessing. As we pray together, she recites a prayer to the hometown saint:

Brigid, embodiment of the Divine Feminine within the Celtic tradition, guide me step by step to the awakening of God in my life. Keep my heart and soul open to the knowledge of your wisdom in my life.[31]

ON THE PATH, WRAPPED IN BRIGID'S MANTLE

Brigid's childhood—and tales of her later life, too—are woven into the fabric of Faughart. Just ask anyone in

Faughart, County Louth

Dundalk about her, and you'll get a couple of stories told with pride. Everybody seems to know her. When Dolores learned about her, she recalls, she "had an instant connection with the idea of the divine feminine. One of the lovely things I learned from one of my teachers was that 'God is good, and he has a great mother.' That great mother is Brigid. That's why we call her *Muire na nGael*, Mary of the Irish. To me, she stands at the heart of our tradition."

At her well in Faughart, near the place of her birth, Brigid's origin stories can inspire us and send us along our own synodal journey. "I know she can teach people—she teaches me—about compassion, about the understanding of interconnectedness, about the absolute unity of the world we live in and the alignment of heaven to earth," says Dolores. "Because everything she did, she did it from that place of alignment and I have learned that from her. I am not nearly there yet but I'm going there."

How can Brigid bring us to that "place of alignment" that Dolores has become aware of, where we can sense our deep connection to the divine? What, in our own lives, may be holding us back? What, in Brigid's example, can help us to move forward?

Chapter 7

KILDARE, COUNTY KILDARE

The City of Brigid: Finding Faith in Kildare

Nineteen nuns at Kildare maintained a fire in St Brigid's honour. Each night one of the nineteen would make sure that the fire remained burning, but every twentieth night Brigid herself performed the task. Brigid was at one with her community. And, this community was a national one. The very earliest writings we have about Brigid suggest that she is the mother of the Irish people, Muire na nGael, Mary of the Irish. What other Irish saint could possibly compete?

"St. Brigid of Kildare: Patron of the Powerless," University College Dublin Library Cultural Heritage Collections[1]

Kildare, County Kildare

You can get from Dublin to Kildare in a little less than an hour. Starting out in a maze of airport traffic, speeding along with commuters, buses, and trucks from every corner of the European Union, the modern superhighway eventually leads you back to winding roads and roundabouts, through the countryside and into Kildare.

It's an old town, dating back to way before Christianity arrived. But it doesn't look as old as you'd expect: it's always been a work in progress, at various stages of destruction and rebuilding. There were constant petty wars, mostly over cattle. Then, in the ninth century, the Vikings showed up. The annals record that in the year 835 Kildare was "plundered by the foreigners...and half the church was burned by them."[2] And that was only the beginning. In the decades that followed, the Vikings returned like clockwork, raiding Kildare's riches and killing its citizens; in 843 they killed the monastery's prior on one of their "plundering excursions," and in 883 they were back, carting "fourteen score of persons into captivity to their ships...besides other valuable property which they carried away."[3]

Long after the Vikings had settled down and turned into respectable Irishmen, the Normans invaded in the twelfth century, all the way from France by way of England. And in the winter of 1315, the famous Scottish warrior, Edward the Bruce, who met his end on the Hill of Faughart, held siege to Kildare Castle. For the people of Kildare, it was one thing after another. By the middle of the 1600s, after the bombardments of the Irish Confederate Wars, which pitted Irish Catholics against British Protestant settlers, the cathedral was in ruins and the town was nearly deserted.[4] Kildare couldn't seem to catch a break. It's a wonder the town survived at all.

Brigid's Mantle

Back in Brigid's day, though, Kildare was a magnificent city. The lure of St. Brigid herself, in the fifth century and beyond, made it a place of pilgrimage and devotion and a respected center of learning. Before that, it had been the site of a pagan shrine venerating Brigid the goddess. At the place where St. Brigid's Cathedral stands now, scholars say, a perpetual fire, tended by a dozen or so young women, burned in honor of the deity of arts, poetry, healing, smithwork, and livestock.[5]

We may never know all the details, but we do know this: sometime in the late fifth century, during "the twilight period when paganism was being superseded by Christianity,"[6] Brigid founded a Christian church and a double monastery of monks and nuns on the site of a druid shrine. Her repurposed holy place sat alongside the ancient oak tree that gave Kildare its name: *Cill Dara*, Irish for the "Church of the Oak." And even when Kildare became Christian, some of the old pagan traditions, like the sacred fire, continued. (When Gerald of Wales visited Ireland in the eleventh century, that fire, tended by nine of St. Brigid's nuns, was still burning.)[7]

Before the Vikings showed up, Kildare had developed into a famous urban center. One of the earliest accounts we have is from the early seventh century, less than a hundred years after St. Brigid's death, when Cogitosus, a monk from her monastery, composed his *Life of Saint Brigid the Virgin*. "On the firm foundation of faith," he writes,

> she established her monastery on the open expanses of the plains of the Mag Liffe [the River Liffey], which is the head of almost all the churches of Ireland and holds the place of honor

Kildare, County Kildare

among all the monasteries of the Irish. Its jurisdiction extends over the whole land of Ireland, from coast to coast...[an] episcopal and feminine see spread...like a fertile vine pushing its burgeoning branches out on all sides....It has always been ruled over by the Archbishop of the Irish and by the abbess, whom all the abbesses of the Irish venerate, by a blessed line of succession and by perpetual rites.[7a]

Legend has it, of course, that its boundaries were drawn by Brigid herself when she spread her cloak over the grassy plains alongside the River Liffey; under her guidance the town grew to prominence. Cogitosus writes of the

great glory of this church and the countless wonders of her monastic city[.] "City" is the right word and is justified by the many people who live there. This city is a great metropolis...where the treasures of kings are kept safe, and it is regarded as being the most excellent on account of its illustrious supremacy.[8]

Today, Kildare is a bustling market town with shops and cafés and mothers pushing strollers and people walking dogs along busy sidewalks. There are parks and playgrounds, takeaway Thai food, and even a Kildare Heritage Center. It's not the shining metropolis that Cogitosus described, but it's a lovely modern community dotted with some ancient landmarks, much like the rest of Ireland. The sacred oak tree is long gone, and so are the pagan shrine and the ancient church of St. Brigid. But there's still the thirteenth-century

Brigid's Mantle

Norman cathedral, with its Sheela-na-gig tucked discreetly under the baptismal font. And beside the imposing granite church—rebuilt a couple of times since the late Middle Ages—are the remains of an oratory where, local legend attests, the sacred fire burned.

Brigid's nuns were disbanded in the wake of the Reformation, as Henry VIII suppressed the monasteries of the British Isles. That's when the sacred fire was put out—but it wasn't put out forever. Brigid was never really forgotten: in 1807, a bishop in County Carlow restored the Brigidine order, whose nuns were tasked with teaching Irish children the faith as the Penal Laws came to an end and the Catholic Church emerged from a century underground. The sisters established convents and schools throughout Ireland and around the world, and finally, in 1993, they returned to their roots in Kildare and relit Brigid's flame there, opening the Solas Bhríde ("Light of Brigid") Center.

It's a beautiful, simple, quiet place, just along Tully Road as you leave town, on land across from the lush, green pastures of Irish National Stud & Gardens, known locally as "Brigid's acres." Set among a grove of oak trees, there are hermitages scattered on the grounds and a labyrinth where you can walk for prayer and meditation. When we arrived at Solas Bhríde, we were greeted by Sister Rita Minehan, a member of the Congregation of St. Brigid and the center's director. "You're most welcome here," she told us, making us feel as though we'd been wrapped in the warmth of the mantle of Brigid herself, the woman who was "joyful and welcoming to all."[9] Ushering us inside, she sat us down in a sunny room, fed us tea and scones, and shared her love for Brigid and her legacy:

Kildare, County Kildare

We're amazed at the numbers of people coming here from all over the world, seeking peace and a deeper meaning in their lives. There are so many extremes today, and so much polarization, just as there were in Brigid's day. But so many people find inspiration in Brigid, who seemed to be interested in social justice throughout her life—she cared for the embarrassed of her time as we hope to notice the untouchables of our own day. She was a woman of deep peace. Everyone seems to resonate with the legend of Brigid with her foot on the sword.[10]

This warm and kindhearted nun had grabbed our attention. Who was this woman with her foot on the sword—and what did peace look like for her? It wasn't a placid, passive life of avoiding conflict, she told us, but one that was powered by the gospel, lit by the fire of the Spirit, and overflowing into care for the "poor and the untouchables." Because Brigid took Christ's message to heart, "answering the needs of the poor, whether it was convenient to do so or not,"[11] she had to run with it, and it set her life in motion. She looked at her world as it was and saw that it didn't match up with the gospel. But that didn't stop her: "She would not," says Brigid scholar Mary Condren, "give in to the norms of a patriarchal spirituality without a fight."[12]

BRIGID AND THE OTHER BISHOPS

Clearly, Brigid wasn't your run-of-the-mill abbess. And whether her episcopal ordination was conferred on purpose or by mistake, she seemed to easily fit into the mold of a bishop. But she was different in one important way: she wasn't much interested in playing by the rules. Nothing got in the way of the life of everyday holiness that she knew God was calling her to. Even as a young girl, her faith led her to extraordinary acts of generosity: she was forever giving away butter and milk and bacon to the poor, then shrugging her shoulders and proclaiming, "It is difficult for me to deprive Christ of his own food."[13] *As a Christian*, she seemed to be asking, *what else could I possibly do?*

It's never easy living with a saint, of course, and Brigid was a thorn in the side of her entire family. Her father Dubthach became so frustrated by her openhandedness that he packed her up in his cart and drove her off to the king of the province of Leinster, offering to sell his daughter as a slave. But while Dubthach was in the castle negotiating her price, Brigid, waiting in the cart, was giving away her father's jeweled sword to a leper who came begging. When the king heard about the incident, he turned down the father's offer. "Truly," he told Dubthach, "this girl can neither be bought nor sold."[14]

That was Brigid in a nutshell. She was a woman on a mission, and from childhood her entire focus was on God. Nothing much changed in the months and years that followed. Against the wishes of her father and brothers, she spurned her society's expectations for women by turning down an offer of marriage, sealing the deal by plucking her eye out of its socket. "It is difficult for me," she explained, "since I have offered up my virginity to God."[15]

As she reached adulthood, she stayed exactly the same: the young girl with complete disregard for her society's norms became a woman who lived her life exactly as

Kildare, County Kildare

she felt called to do. It's little wonder that she became such a powerful (and unconventional) abbess. And it's no wonder at all that, ordained a bishop, she took her rightful place among the other bishops and all the luminaries of the early Irish church. Why not? She certainly seemed to have the divine seal of approval: when she was consecrated by Bishop Mel, after all, "a fiery column arose from her head."[16]

Just as she'd had no regard for the concept of private ownership, as an abbess and as a bishop, she was unfazed by ecclesiastical rules and regulations. Unlike the more secluded women of her day—and certainly unlike other nuns—nothing seemed to keep her down, or even to tie her to her monastery in Kildare. She had places to go and people to heal and a gospel to preach, so she was always on the move. Cogitosus writes that after she'd spent a night praying with a nun, giving her a new cow and restoring her broken loom, she got right back on the road. "Her miracles performed, St. Brigid bade farewell to those living in the house and, cheerfully setting out, continued on her journey in the manner of a bishop."[17]

She was, it seems, much in demand: she attended a "congregation of the Synod of Leinster,"[18] and at the home of a nobleman, she and "the other bishops" were "welcomed with respect and kindness and entertained."[19] She was invited to "go and address twenty-seven Leinster saints in a single gathering."[20]

Not only did Brigid travel "in the manner of a bishop," she acted as a bishop in other ways too. From her "episcopal and feminine see,"[21] she seems to have ruled what amounted to a sizeable diocese, where she also served as a priest and spiritual adviser. For that, she incurred the ire of the church in later centuries, writes preeminent Brigid scholar Mary Condren:

> Although the image of Brigid the saint may have come down to us as one of an obedient, if spirited, woman, in the "Lives" of Brigid there is evidence, even apart from the possible "vestal virgin" origins of Kildare, that made Brigid's spirituality problematic for the early Irish church.[22]

Bishops and church historians can't, of course, go back in time and change what Brigid may have done in the past. But they can—and often do—suppress any mention of it in official documents. This was one of their biggest concerns, writes Condren:

> Brigid was even credited with celebrating what amounts to an early Irish Eucharist.... There must have been some historical basis for the claims.... The fact that these claims surrounded Brigid is itself a highly significant indication of early Irish religiosity. The political significance of some of these stories has been apparent to the church for some time, and for this reason attempts have been made to suppress the most controversial elements. This can be seen in the story of Brigid's ordination as a bishop [which appears in seventh- and eighth-century hagiography but disappears in the writings published in later centuries].[23]

She preached homilies—even the king of Leinster came to listen to her preaching—and she was involved in liturgical celebrations, too.[24] People hearing these stories in the early church didn't seem to have a problem accepting that this might indeed have happened. Although misogyny was imported from Rome along with Christianity, in Ireland, Condren points out, "no difference was then made between man and woman....Women...assumed to themselves sacramental functions."[25]

For the most part, Brigid's fellow church leaders didn't seem to have much of a problem with it, either. The bishops welcomed her to their midst and treated her as a peer. She entertained them at Kildare, providing miraculous supplies of food and changing water into "beer with the fragrance of wine."[26] She was even called upon to resolve disputes among the hierarchy.[27] In one story, she went a great distance to hear Patrick preach, falling asleep during his sermon while she received visions directly from God. (When she woke up, Patrick mansplained the visions to her.)[28]

She took on other liturgical functions, too. At a Maundy Thursday Eucharist, she assumed one of the ceremonial duties of a bishop, "washing the feet of the old men and the feeble folk who were in the church. Four of the sick people there were a consumptive man, a madman, a blind man, and a leper. Brigid washed the feet of the four, and they were straightway healed from every disease that was on them."[29]

Even if she was just a lowly nun, she was always at home in high places. Legend has it that many of the renowned early Irish saints were Brigid's peers and confidants, though Brigid, time and again, was shown to be infinitely superior. Take Brendan, for example. He was a sixth-century founder of churches and monasteries, known for his fantastic ocean voyages, who shows up from time to time in the stories of Brigid's life. In one incident, he arrives unexpectedly at Kildare from the west of Ireland, and as they enter the monastery together, "Brigid hangs her cloak on a sunbeam and when Brendan tries to do the same it falls immediately to the ground—a story clearly designed to make Brendan look ridiculous and to indicate Brigid's superiority."[30]

Then Brigid hears Brendan's confession (another priestly task), after which he listens to hers. In a bit of holy bragging, Brendan attests that it's not unusual for him "to go over seven ridges without giving my mind to God." But Brigid one-ups him: "Since I first gave my mind to God," she declares, "I never took it off him at all."[31] Brigid clearly holds her own among the panoply of male leaders of the early Irish church. Even more remarkable, she was in charge of a liturgical life at Kildare that wasn't exactly orthodox—and she seems to have resisted calls to bring it into line with Rome. As Condren points out:

> The rites practiced at Kildare were clearly problematic for the early church—so problematic that several stories are told about Brigid's persistent but unsuccessful attempts to get a Roman "Ordo"…that ensured orthodox worship throughout the Christian church.…One of her messengers deliberately falsified the copy of the "Ordo," which explained why the rites at Kildare were different from those practiced elsewhere.…The storytellers were anxious to tell us that Brigid made every effort to get the Roman liturgy—which indicates to us at least that what she did use was far from being acceptable and orthodox.[32]

Kildare, County Kildare

You don't have to read too far behind the lines to see that Brigid was deeply involved in the liturgy at her monastery—and that she did things her way. She may—or may not—have celebrated the Eucharist, and we may never know exactly what the liturgy looked and sounded like at her monastery. Some scholars think the rites she used may have been brought to Ireland by Celtic invaders. But the record shows that Brigid knew that the Kildare rites weren't quite in line with Rome. Her emissaries came back to Ireland empty-handed again and again, "having promptly 'forgotten' what they had been told," and it took a blind boy with a perfect memory to finally bring the official Ordo back to Kildare.[33]

In her monastery at Kildare, Brigid was more than a quiet, obedient nun. She was a powerful spiritual leader who was clearly engaged in guiding the souls under her care. Down the road at her holy well, she wielded power of a very different kind.

BRIGID'S HOLY WELL AT KILDARE

A mile or so from Solas Bhríde, past the horse pastures of the National Stud and Gardens, past farms and houses, a small sign directs you to *Tobar Bríde*, St. Brigid's Well. Down a path and over a footbridge, there's a quiet, mystical place, bounded by a wooden fence and surrounded by farmland. The path brings you face to face with Brigid the country girl: first with a life-size statue of a young, vigorous woman, then through the deep sense of peace that connects you with the girl who once herded livestock here and "kept the calves fat."[34] According to Sister Rita, "Tradition holds that St. Brigid kept her cows here, prayed here, and may have made butter by the stream."[35] In the early days of the church, people were baptized here and later—during the eighteenth-century penal days—they came here in secret to attend Mass.

It's easy to feel Brigid's presence here, fifteen hundred years later. The bronze-green statue looks over the scene: with her crozier in one hand and her flaming torch in the other, Brigid seems to be "striding forth with purpose and intent,"[36] welcoming (and even challenging) visitors who enter into her space. You can imagine Brigid in this place, among the grassy fields, the bushes and trees, with the sound of flowing water and birdsong. Today there are clooties and other offerings on the trees; similar trinkets were probably here in Brigid's day, too.

Like so much of Kildare, this well, sacred to Brigid the Christian saint, was likely also sacred to her predecessor, Brigid the goddess. The Brennemans write in *Crossing the Circle at the Holy Wells of Ireland* that the well

> maintains much of the early mother goddess symbolism, especially that of her relationship to the Lord of the Otherworld as divine smith and lord of the oak grove...just outside the town of Kildare....This is her country, her place....There are several unique features of this well that link St. Bridgid to the goddess Brigid....Near the spring itself, which is located on the edge of a field, is a stone tablet standing upright. On one side is incised a St Brigid's cross, whose swastika form symbolizes the fiery sun and retains continu-

Kildare, County Kildare

ity with the goddess's association with the sacred smith and his fire. On the other side is incised a Christian cross, bringing together or syncretizing [the old religion and the new one].[37]

Just a few steps on, the Brennemans point out, you'll encounter another aspect of Brigid: her connection to womanhood and fertility, emphasizing her role as "the Mary of the Gael" and midwife to Mary. Within the spring, the water passes through a couple of stone tubes, flowing out their other ends, reminding visitors of a woman's breasts with milk flowing out to her children:

> What we find at the ancient cult center of Brigid today is that this Earth Goddess of Kildare has metamorphosed into a Christian saint, St Brigid, who has retained in her attributes and cult objects, including her well, many of her previous powers. She remains present in the earth, through which she heals by means of her holy well outside the town; and at that well we see the confluence of the symbolisms of fecundity, nurturing, and healing through the identification of milk and water as the spring flows through the stone "cows."[38]

Tradition has it that this water was used for early Christian baptisms. The water flows into a circular well, bounded by granite stones, in which local people have occasionally spotted a fish—which is taken to mean that Brigid has heard and answered your prayers. But fish or no fish, people come here with their prayers and petitions, or just to sit in quiet and peace for a little while.

Some of the pilgrims perform the "rounds," walking sunwise, in the ancient Irish tradition, and saying certain prayers at each of the stone "stations." They might recite a decade of the rosary at each stone, or they might meditate on scripture passages that are meaningful to them. Sister Rita provides a "pattern" that visitors can follow at each of the stations,[39] or you can make up your own. Just the act of being here in this peaceful place is a meaningful spiritual experience.

The final stop on the rounds, of course, is the circular well, where the water, after flowing underground for a few yards, reappears. Visitors bless themselves with it and scoop it up into bottles to take back and bless their homes and families. Maybe there's a fish—or maybe not—but in this quiet, peaceful place, there's a long tradition of healing, of body and soul, heart and mind. *A naoimh Brhid, gui oriann.* St. Brigid, pray for us.

ON THE PATH, WRAPPED IN BRIGID'S MANTLE

Brigid lived a life of "holy disobedience." A young girl—and a woman—of implacable will, she forged ahead and did what she thought was right, regardless of what anyone in authority may have told her. Rita Minehan writes in *Rekindling the Flame*:

> Brigid is an inspiration for many today in their efforts to promote the equal dignity of women

Kildare, County Kildare

and men in church and society. She blazed a trail for female leadership in fifth-century Ireland. We can still hear a female voice coming from a patriarchal world. She and the women who succeeded her, the subsequent abbesses of Kildare, were arguably the most powerful women in Ireland, for many centuries.[40]

What makes disobedience "holy"? And how can Brigid's experience help us decide?

Is it fair to call Brigid, who lived in a completely different time and place, a feminist? How does feminism play out in the church today? Does Brigid offer us an example or an inspiration?

Brigid seemed to be unconcerned that worship at her monastery wasn't exactly orthodox and didn't conform with worship in the rest of the universal church. Why do you think uniformity of worship might be important? In what ways do you think it might help—or hinder—a holy creativity?

NOTES

INTRODUCTION

1. A note about spelling: there are many different ways to spell the name of the saint of Kildare, from Brigit to Bridget to Bride. For the sake of simplicity, I've chosen to use the spelling *Brigid* throughout this book, including in quotes from other sources.

2. Brigidine Sisters, "The Story of Brigid," Solas Bhríde Center and Hermitages, Kildare, County Kildare, https://solasbhride.ie/the-story-of-brigid/.

3. Brigidine Sisters, "Story of Brigid."

4. "St. Brigid," National Folklore Collection, roll number 10262, https://www.duchas.ie/en/cbes/4922062/4848882/500975.

5. Lisa M. Bitel, *Land of Women: Tales of Sex and Gender from Early Ireland* (Ithaca, NY: Cornell University Press, 1996), 11.

6. Noel Kissane, *Saint Brigid of Kildare: Life, Legend and Cult* (Dublin: Open Air, 2017), 22n6.

7. Christina Harrington, *Women in a Celtic Church: Ireland 450–1150* (New York: Oxford University Press, 2002), 26–27.

8. Walter L. Brenneman and Mary G. Brenneman, *Crossing the Circle at the Holy Wells of Ireland* (Charlottesville: University Press of Virginia, 1995), 26.

9. Brenneman and Brenneman, *Crossing the Circle*, 24.
10. Brenneman and Brenneman, *Crossing the Circle*, 24.
11. Mary Condren, *The Serpent and the Goddess: Women, Religion, and Power in Celtic Ireland* (San Francisco: Harper & Row, 1989), 49.
12. Condren, *Serpent and the Goddess*, 66.
13. Condren, *Serpent and the Goddess*, 76.
14. Anne Thayer, personal interview, April 11, 2018.
15. Thomas J. Heffernan, *Sacred Biography: Saints and Their Biographers in the Middle Ages* (New York: Oxford University Press, 1988), 20.
16. "The Irish Life of Brigit," in *Celtic Spirituality*, ed. and trans. Oliver Davies, Classics of Western Spirituality (Mahwah, NJ: Paulist Press, 1999), 145.
17. Gary Macy, *The Hidden History of Women's Ordination: Female Clergy in the Medieval West* (New York: Oxford University Press, 2008), 54.
18. Aideen M. O'Leary, "Contested Consecrations and the Pursuit of Ecclesiastical Independence in Scotland and Ireland in the Early 1120s, *North American Journal of Celtic studies* 2, no. 2 (2018): 158.
19. O'Leary, "Contested Consecrations," 158.
20. Davies, "The Irish Life of Brigit," 145.
21. Kissane, *Saint Brigid of Kildare*, 121.
22. Kissane, *Saint Brigid of Kildare*, 121.
23. Kissane, *Saint Brigid of Kildare*, 122.
24. Condren, Serpent and the Goddess, 110.
25. "The Life of St. Brigit the Virgin by Cogitosus," in Davies, *Celtic Spirituality*, 126.
26. Dolores Whelan, personal interview, Dundalk, Co. Louth, April 27, 2023.
27. Brenneman and Brenneman, *Crossing the Circle*, 122–23.
28. Mary Seaborne O'Connell, "The Brigid and Mary Stories in Gaelic Culture: 'And Anyway She Was Always Going

Notes

About with the Mother of God,'" in *Celts in Legends and Reality: Papers from the Sixth Australian Conference of Celtic Studies*, ed. Pamela O'Neil (Sydney: UNSW, July 2007), 199–220, https://unsworks.unsw.edu.au/entities/publication/d516054e-029f-45a6-932b-5e8fd2e7ddd9.

29. Lawrence J. Taylor, *Occasions of Faith: An Anthropology of Irish Catholics* (Philadelphia: University of Pennsylvania Press, 1995), 65.

30. Meg Byrne, personal interview, Cliffoney, County Sligo, April 25, 2023.

CHAPTER 1

1. Lady Augusta Gregory, *A Book of Saints and Wonders* (North Haven, CT: First Rate Publishers, 2014).

2. Bryan MacMahon, *A Guide to Ballyheigue* (Ballyheigue, Ireland: Ballyheigue Parish History and Heritage Group, 2013), 9.

3. "St. Bernadette," The Lourdes Center, Boston, accessed March 2, 2024, https://www.lourdescenter.org/bernadette.html.

4. Celeste Ray, "The Sacred and the Body Politic at Ireland's Holy Wells," *ISSJ* 62, nos. 205–6 (September–December 2011): 276.

5. Ray, "Sacred and the Body Politic," 277.

6. Lawrence J. Taylor, *Occasions of Faith: An Anthropology of Irish Catholics* (Philadelphia: University of Pennsylvania Press, 1995), 200.

7. Mary Seaborne O'Connell, "The Brigid and Mary Stories in Gaelic Culture: 'And Anyway She Was Always Going About with the Mother of God,'" in *Celts in Legends and Reality: Papers from the Sixth Australian Conference on Celtic Studies*, ed. Pamela O'Neil (Sydney: UNSW, 2007), 199–220, https://unsworks.unsw.edu.au/entities/publication/d516054e-029f-45a6-932b-5e8fd2e7ddd9.

8. Cara Delay, "The Devotional Revolution on the Local Level: Parish Life in Post-famine Ireland," *U.S. Catholic Historian* 22, no. 3 (Summer 2004): 41–60, https://www.jstor.org/stable/25154919.

9. "The Irish Life of Brigit," in *Celtic Spirituality*, ed. and trans. Oliver Davies, Classics of Western Spirituality (Mahwah, NJ: Paulist Press, 1999), 143.

10. O'Connell, "Brigid and Mary Stories," 199–220.

11. Joel D. S. Rasmussen, Judith Wolfe, and Johannes Zachhuber, eds., *The Oxford Handbook of Nineteenth-Century Christian Thought* (Oxford: Oxford University Press, 2017), 582.

12. O'Connell, "Brigid and Mary Stories in Gaelic Culture," 19.

13. Lisa Godson, "Charting the Material Culture of the 'Devotional Revolution': The Advertising Register of the *Irish Catholic Directory*, 1837–96," *Proceedings of the Royal Irish Academy* 116C (April 30, 2015): 1–30.

14. Ann Wilson, "Irish Catholic Fiction of the Early Twentieth Century: The Power of Imagery," *Iris Éireannach Nua* 18, no. 1 (2014): 30–49, http://www.jstor.org/stable/24624285.

15. Amanda Clarke, "Cream Pies and Crubeens: Pattern Day in Ballyheigue," Holy Wells of Cork and Kerry, September 15, 2019, https://holywellscorkandkerry.com/2019/09/15/cream-pies-crubeens-pattern-day-in-ballyheigue/.

16. Walter L. Brenneman and Mary G. Brenneman, *Crossing the Circle at the Holy Wells of Ireland* (Charlottesville: University Press of Virginia, 1995), 113.

17. "Ballyheigue," Diocese of Kerry, St. Mary's Church, accessed March 5, 2024, https://www.dioceseofkerry.ie/parish/ballyheigue/.

18. Gregory, *Book of Saints and Wonders*.

19. Taylor, *Occasions of Faith*, 65.

20. Brenneman and Brenneman, *Crossing the Circle*, 110.

Notes

21. MacMahon, *Guide to Ballyheigue*, 62.
22. Amanda Clarke, email correspondence, May 2024.
23. Noel Kissane, *Saint Brigid of Kildare: Life, Legend and Cult* (Dublin: Open Air, 2017), 134n134.
24. "Holy Wells," National Folklore Collection, roll number 2493, https://www.duchas.ie/en/cbes/4666610/4666528/4682787.
25. "St Dahalan og Ballyheighue (Baile Thaidhg) agus Tobar na Súl," National Folklore Collection, https://www.duchas.ie/en/cbes/4706337/4703931/4743273.
26. Brenneman and Brenneman, *Crossing the Circle*, 90.

CHAPTER 2

1. Walter L. and Mary G. Brenneman, *Crossing the Circle at the Holy Wells of Ireland* (Charlottesville: University Press of Virginia, 1995), 16.
2. Barbara Freitag, *Sheela-na-Gigs: Unravelling an Enigma* (New York: Routledge, 2004), 107.
3. Freitag, *Sheela-na-Gigs*, 107.
4. Patrick Logan, *The Holy Wells of Ireland* (Gerrards Cross, UK: Colin Smythe, 1980), 36–37.
5. Edmond O'Donoghue, "A Story of Cures at Castlemagner Holy Well," Castlemagner Historical Society, October 20, 2016, https://castlemagner-his-soc.com/a-story-of-cures-at-castlemagner-holy-well/.
6. Mary C. Earle and Sylvia Maddox, *Holy Companions: Spiritual Practices from the Celtic Saints* (Harrisburg, PA: Morehouse Publishing, 2004), 21.
7. Mary Condren, *The Serpent and the Goddess: Women, Religion, and Power in Celtic Ireland* (San Francisco: Harper & Row, 1989), 65.

8. Miriam Robbins Dexter, "The Sheela Na Gigs, Sexuality, and the Goddess in Ancient Ireland," *Irish Journal of Feminist Studies in Religion* 4, no. 2 (2002): 50–75.

9. Freitag, *Sheela-na-Gigs*, 106.

10. Edmond O'Donoghue, "8th Century Church in Subulter," Castlemagner Historical Society, September 30, 2017, https://castlemagner-his-soc.com/8th-century-church-in-subulter/.

11. O'Donoghue, "Story of Cures."

12. Brenneman and Brenneman, *Crossing the Circle*, 13.

13. Brenneman and Brenneman, *Crossing the Circle*, 4.

14. Brenneman and Brenneman, *Crossing the Circle*, 4.

15. Brenneman and Brenneman, *Crossing the Circle*, 33–34.

16. Jenny Stevens, "Big Vagina Energy: The Return of the Sheela na Gig," *The Guardian*, March 8, 2021, https://www.theguardian.com/world/2021/mar/08/big-vagina-energy-the-return-of-the-sheela-na-gig.

17. Séamas Ó Catháin, "Hearth-Prayers and Other Traditions of Brigid: Celtic Goddess and Holy Woman," *Journal of the Royal Society of Antiquaries of Ireland* 122 (1992): 12–34, https://www.jstor.org/stable/25509020.

18. Louise Nugent, *Journeys of Faith: Stories of Pilgrimage from Medieval Ireland* (Dublin: Columba Books, 2020), 245.

19. Starr Goode, *Sheela na Gig: The Dark Goddess of Sacred Power* (Rochester, VT: Inner Traditions, 2016), 70.

20. Goode, *Sheela na Gig*, 170.

21. Brenneman and Brenneman, *Crossing the Circle*, 33.

22. Della Hooke, "Christianity and the 'Sacred Tree,'" in *Trees and Timber in the Anglo-Saxon World*, ed. Michael D. J. Brintley and Michael J. Shapland (Oxford: Oxford University Press, 2013), 228–50.

23. Brenneman and Brenneman, *Crossing the Circle*, 81.

24. Condren, *Serpent and the Goddess*, 124.

25. James Mackey, "Preface," in *Celtic Spirituality*, ed. and trans. Oliver Davies, Classics of Western Spirituality (Mahwah, NJ: Paulist Press, 1999), xvi.

Notes

26. Earle and Maddox, *Holy Companions*, 21.
27. Noel Kissane, *Saint Brigid of Kildare: Life, Legend and Cult* (Dublin: Open Air, 2017), 38.

CHAPTER 3

1. *On the Life of St. Brigit*, trans. Whitley Stokes, Corpus of Electronic Texts, University College, Cork, Ireland, https://celt.ucc.ie/published/T201010.html, 85.
2. Roseanne Schot, "Uisneach Midi a medón Érenn: A Prehistoric 'Cult Centre' and 'Royal Site' in Co. Westmeath," *Journal of Irish Archaeology* 15 (2006): 39.
3. Schot, "Uisneach Midi a medon Erenn," 41.
4. "Religious," National Folklore Collection, roll number 9409, https://www.duchas.ie/en/cbes/5009113/4988068?HighlightText=killare&Route=stories&SearchLanguage=ga.
5. "Holy Wells," National Folklore Collection, roll number 9409, https://www.duchas.ie/en/cbes/5009113/4988089?HighlightText=killare&Route=stories&SearchLanguage=ga.
6. Ruth Illington, personal interview, Mullingar, Co. Westmeath, April 20, 2023.
7. "The Irish Life of Brigit," in *Celtic Spirituality*, ed. and trans. Oliver Davies (Mahwah, NJ: Paulist Press, 1999), 30.
8. Davies, "Irish Life of Brigit," 31.
9. Davies, "Irish Life of Brigit," 40.
10. Davies, "Irish Life of Brigit," 41.
11. Davies, "Irish Life of Brigit," 43.
12. "The Life of St. Brigit the Virgin by Cogitosus," in Davies, *Celtic Spirituality*, 129.
13. Davies, "Life of St. Brigit," 131.
14. Davies, "Life of St. Brigit," 135.
15. Illington, personal interview.

16. Brigidine Sisters, "Our Patroness," https://brigidine.org.au/about-us/our-patroness/.

17. Christina Harrington, *Women in a Celtic Church: Ireland 450–1150* (New York: Oxford University Press, 2002), 185.

18. Mary Condren, *The Serpent and the Goddess: Women, Religion, and Power in Celtic Ireland* (San Francisco: Harper & Row, 1989), 76–77.

19. Davies, "Irish Life of Brigit," 145.

20. "Our Holy Wells," National Folklore Collection, roll number 7444, https://www.duchas.ie/en/cbes/5009112/4987887/5130381?HighlightText=killare&Route=stories&SearchLanguage=ga.

21. "Kildare and St. Brigid's Well," National Folklore Collection, roll number 1880, https://www.duchas.ie/en/cbes/5009104/4987063.

22. Illington, personal interview.

23. Lisa Bitel, *Landscape with Two Saints: How Genovefa of Paris and Brigid of Kildare Built Christianity in Barbarian Europe* (Oxford: Oxford University Press, 2009), 6.

24. Rita Minehan, *Rekindling the Flame: A Pilgrimage in the Footsteps of Brigid of Kildare* (Kildare, Ireland: Solas Bhríde Community, 1999), 49.

25. Pope Francis, "Instrumentum laboris" of the 16th Ordinary General Assembly of the Synod of Bishops, June 20, 2023, https://press.vatican.va/content/salastampa/en/bollettino/pubblico/2023/06/20/230620e.html.

CHAPTER 4

1. "Ultan's Hymn," in *Celtic Spirituality*, ed. and trans. Oliver Davies, Classics of Western Spirituality (Mahwah, NJ: Paulist Press), 121.

Notes

2. Walter L. Brenneman and Mary G. Brenneman, *Crossing the Circle at the Holy Wells of Ireland* (Charlottesville: University Press of Virginia, 1995), 4.

3. Pius Murray, personal interview, Corofin, County Clare, September 25, 2018.

4. Dudoit Raiche, "Liturgical Catechesis: A Method with Constitutive Elements," *International Journal of Evangelization and Catechetics* 1, no. 1 (Winter 2020): 19–43, https://doi.org/10.1353/jec.2020.0000.

5. Edward Sri, "The Origins of the Rosary," St. Anthony Messenger, June 2017, https://www.franciscanmedia.org/st-anthony-messenger/the-origins-of-the-rosary.

6. Piero Marini, "The Way of the Cross," Office for the Liturgical Celebrations of the Supreme Pontiff, https://www.vatican.va/news_services/liturgy/documents/ns_lit_doc_via-crucis_en.html.

7. *On the Life of St. Brigit*, trans Whitley Stokes, Corpus of Electronic Texts, University College, Cork, Ireland, https://celt.ucc.ie/published/T201010.html, 15.

8. Dolores Whelan, personal interview, Dundalk, County Louth, April 23, 2023.

9. Lady Augusta Gregory, "She Remembers the Poor," in *A Book of Saints and Wonders* (North Haven, CT: First Rate Publishers, 2014).

10. Celeste Ray, "The Sacred and Body Politic and Ireland's Holy Wells," *International Social Science Journal* 62 (September–December 2011): 283.

11. Mary Condren, email correspondence, March 27, 2018.

12. Ray, "Sacred and Body Politic," 283.

CHAPTER 5

1. Lady Augusta Gregory, "The Things Brigid Wished For," in *A Book of Saints and Wonders* (North Haven, CT: First Rate Publishers, 2014).

2. "The Cliffoney Pattern," National Folklore Collection, roll number 13882, https://www.duchas.ie/en/cbes/4701657/4690153.

3. Séamas Ó Catháin, "The Festival of Brigit the Holy Woman," in "Essays in Honour of James Patrick Carney," *Celtica* 23 (1999): 231–60, https://www.dias.ie/celt/celtica/celtica-volume-23.

4. "The Irish Life of Brigit," in *Celtic Spirituality*, ed. and trans. Oliver Davies (Mahwah, NJ: Paulist Press), 145.

5. Mary Condren, *The Serpent and the Goddess: Women, Religion, and Power in Celtic Ireland* (San Francisco: Harper & Row, 1989), 30–31.

6. Condren, *Serpent and the Goddess*, 26.

7. Davies, "Irish Life of Brigit," 145.

8. Gary Macy, *The Hidden History of Women's Ordination: Female Clergy in the Medieval West* (Oxford: Oxford University Press, 2007), 54. Italics mine.

9. Meg Byrne, personal interview, Cliffoney, County Sligo, April 24, 2023.

10. Martin Byrne, "From Cliffoney to Crosna: The Story of Fr. Michael O'Flanagan," Father Michael O'Flanagan History and Heritage Center, http://www.carrowkeel.com/frof/froflanagan.html.

11. David Wood, "Gabhaim molta Bríde," *Song of the Isles* (blog), February 1, 2014, https://songoftheisles.com/2014/02/01/gabhaim-molta-bride/.

12. Noel Kissane, *Saint Brigid of Kildare: Life, Legend and Cult* (Dublin: Open Air, 2017), 23.

13. Meg Byrne, personal interview, Cliffoney, County Sligo, April 24, 2024.

Notes

CHAPTER 6

1. "The Life of St. Brigit the Virgin by Cogitosus," in *Celtic Spirituality*, ed. and trans. Oliver Davies (Mahwah, NJ: Paulist Press, 1999), 124.

2. Dolores Whelan, "Brigid of Faughart: Wise Guide for Modern Soul-Seekers," *Brigid of Faughart Festival* (blog), January 6, 2022, https://www.brigidoffaughart.ie/brigid-of-faughart-wise-guide-for-modern-soul-seekers-by-dolores-whelan/.

3. Mary Condren, *The Serpent and the Goddess: Women, Religion, and Power in Celtic Ireland* (San Francisco: Harper & Row, 1989), 76.

4. Stanley Howard, "Faughart, County Louth, and Its Surroundings," *Journal of the Royal Society of Antiquaries of Ireland* 36, no. 1 (1906): 59–75, https://www.jstor.org/stable/25507498.

5. "Saint Brigid: Incidents from Her Life," National Folklore Collection, roll number 12357, https://www.duchas.ie/en/cbes/4758463/4746391.

6. "Saint Brigid's Well," National Folklore Collection, https://www.duchas.ie/en/cbes/5070826/5068044.

7. *On the Life of St. Brigit*, trans. Whitley Stokes, Corpus of Electronic Texts, University College, Cork, Ireland, https://celt.ucc.ie/published/T201010/index.html, 57.

8. *On the Life of St. Brigit*, 55.

9. *On the Life of St. Brigit*, 7.

10. *On the Life of St. Brigit*, 57.

11. Condren, *Serpent and the Goddess*, 177.

12. *On the Life of St. Brigit*, 57.

13. *On the Life of St. Brigit*, 57.

14. "The Irish Life of Brigit," in Davies, *Celtic Spirituality*, 140.

15. Amy Sherwood, "An Bó Bheannaithe: Cattle Symbolism in Traditional Irish Folklore, Myth, and Archaeology," *PSU*

McNair Scholars Online Journal 3, no. 1 (2009), https://doi.org/10.15760/mcnair.2009.189.

16. Lady Augusta Gregory, "Brigid in Her Young Youth," in *A Book of Saints and Wonders* (North Haven, CT: First Rate Publishers, 2014).

17. Davies, "Life of St. Brigit," 128.

18. Davies, "Life of St. Brigit," 124.

19. Davies, "Irish Life of Brigit," 134.

20. Davies, "Irish Life of Brigit," 144.

21. Lisa M. Bitel, "Body of a Saint, Story of a Goddess: Origins of the Brigidine Tradition," *Textual Practice* 16, no. 2 (2002): 209–28, https://doi.org/10.1080/09502360210141466.

22. "St. Brigid's Stream," National Folklore Collection, roll number 16719, https://www.duchas.ie/en/cbes/5008821/4958964/5071328.

23. Dolores Whelan, personal interview, Faughart, Co. Louth, April 2023.

24. "Faughart, Co. Louth: The Hill of Heroes, Saints, Battles and Boundaries," *Archaeology Ireland* (2007), https://www.jstor.org/stable/archirel.37.1.

25. Gill Boazman, "The Material Culture of Self-Promotion: The Conaille Muirthemne Kings and the Ecclesiastical Site of Faughart, County Louth," *Journal of the County Louth Archaeological and Historical Society* 28, no. 3 (2015): 327–50, https://www.jstor.org/stable/44508599.

26. "Faughart, Co. Louth."

27. Whelan interview.

28. "St. Brigid's Stream," National Folklore Collection, roll number 16719, https://www.duchas.ie/en/cbes/5008821/4958965.

29. Patrick Logan, *The Holy Wells of Ireland* (Gerrards Cross, UK: Colin Smythe, 1980), 53.

30. Whelan interview.

31. Whelan interview.

Notes

CHAPTER 7

1. Elva Johnston, "St. Brigid of Kildare: Patron of the Powerless," *University College Dublin Library Cultural Heritage Collections* (blog), January 25, 2018, https://ucdculturalheritagecollections.com/2018/01/25/st-bridgit-of-kildare-patron-of-the-powerless/.
2. Donnchadh Ó Corráin, "Vikings in Ireland and Scotland in the Ninth Century," *Peritia* 12 (1998): 296–339, https://celt.ucc.ie/Vikings%20in%20Scotland%20and%20Ireland.pdf; *Annals of the Four Masters*, trans. John O'Donovan, Corpus of Electronic Texts (Cork, Ireland: University College, 2008), M835.12 and M843.11, https://celt.ucc.ie/published/T100005F/index.html.
3. *Annals of the Four Masters*, M843.11.
4. "History of Kildare Town," The County Kildare Federation of Local History Groups, accessed March 18, 2024, https://kildarelocalhistory.ie/kildare/history-of-kildare-town/.
5. Noel Kissane, *Saint Brigid of Kildare: Life, Legend, and Cult* (Dublin: Open Air, 2017), 81.
6. Kissane, *Saint Brigid of Kildare*, 81.
7. Oliver Davies, trans., with Thomas O'Loughlin, "The Sources: Introduction to the Translated Texts," in *Celtic Spirituality* (Mahwah, NJ: Paulist Press, 2000), 26.
7a. Davies with O'Loughlin, "The Life of St. Brigit the Virgin by Cogitosus," in *Celtic Spirituality*, 122.
8. Davies, "Life of St. Brigit," 127.
9. Rita Minehan, CSB, personal interview, Kildare, County Kildare, April 2023.
10. Minehan interview.
11. Davies, "Life of St. Brigit," 128.
12. Mary Condren, *The Serpent and the Goddess: Women, Religion, and Power in Celtic Ireland* (San Francisco: Harper & Row, 1989), 75.
13. Davies, "Irish Life of Brigit," 142–43.
14. Davies, "Irish Life of Brigit," 143.

15. Davies, "Irish Life of Brigit," 143–44.
16. Davies, "Irish Life of Brigit," 145.
17. Davies, "Life of St. Brigit the Virgin," 133.
18. *Vita Prima*, 8.
19. Davies, "Irish Life of Brigit," 148.
20. Davies, "Irish Life of Brigit," 142.
21. Davies, "Life of St. Brigit," 122.
22. Condren, *Serpent and the Goddess*, 74.
23. Condren, *Serpent and the Goddess*, 76.
24. *Vita Prima*, 13.
25. Condren, *Serpent and the Goddess*, 98.
26. Davies, "Irish Life of Brigit," 147.
27. Davies, "Irish Life of Brigit," 152.
28. *Vita Prima*, 11.
29. *Vita Prima*, 10.
30. Condren, *Serpent and the Goddess*, 75.
31. *Vita Prima*, 15.
32. Condren, *Serpent and the Goddess*, 68.
33. Condren, *Serpent and the Goddess*, 68.
34. *Vita Prima*, 8.
35. Rita Minehan, *Rekindling the Flame: A Pilgrimage in the Footsteps of Brigid of Kildare* (Kildare, Ireland: Solas Bhríde Community, new edition, 2022), 45.
36. Minehan, *Rekindling the Flame*, 46.
37. Walter L. Brenneman and Mary G. Brenneman, *Crossing the Circle at the Holy Wells of Ireland* (Charlottesville: University Press of Virginia, 1995), 98.
38. Brenneman and Brenneman, *Crossing the Circle*, 98–99.
39. Minehan, *Rekindling the Flame*, 46–53.
40. Minehan, *Rekindling the Flame*, 62.

INDEX

Ballyduff, Co. Kerry, xxxii, 3, 9, 12, 13, 93, 94, 95
Ballyheigue, Co. Kerry, 1, 2, 3, 8, 9, 12, 93, 94, 95
Bethu Brigte, 55
bile, 26, 27, 38
Bitel, Lisa, xxi, 39
Brehon law, xxi
Brendan, Saint, 19, 83, 84
Brenneman, Mary, xxii, 9, 13, 14, 22, 23, 26, 27, 44, 86, 87, 91, 92, 94, 95, 96, 99
Brenneman, Walter, xxii, 9, 13, 14, 22, 23, 26, 27, 44, 86, 87, 91, 92, 94, 95, 96, 99
Brigid cross, xxii, 22, 35, 45, 53, 54, 55, 86
Brú na Bóinne, xx
Byrne, Meg, xv, xxxi, xxxiv, 53, 55, 56, 58, 93, 100

Castlemagner, Co. Cork, xx, xxvii, xxxii, 14, 15, 18, 19, 20, 21, 23, 24, 25, 26, 27, 28, 29
Castlemagner Historical Society, 21, 95, 96
Catholic Emancipation Act, 7
Clarke, Amanda, 10, 94, 95
Cliffoney, Co. Sligo, x, xxx, 51, 52, 54, 55, 56, 57, 58, 93
Condren, Mary, xxiii, xxiv, 19, 28, 49, 79, 82, 83, 84

Delay, Cara, 5, 94
druid, xx, xxi, 19, 21, 22, 26, 32, 33, 39, 44, 54, 58, 61, 63, 65, 66, 67, 68, 76
Dundalk, Co. Louth, xv, xxvii, xxix, 60, 62, 69, 71, 73, 92, 99

Earle, Mary, 18, 73, 92, 97, 99

Faughart, Co. Louth, x, xxx, xxxiii, 60, 61, 62, 64, 66, 67, 68, 69, 71, 72, 73, 75, 101, 102
filli, xxi, 54
folklore collection, 11, 15, 32, 36, 38, 52, 62, 71, 95, 97, 98, 100, 101, 102
Freitag, Barbara, 17, 20, 24, 95, 96

Gabhaim Molta Bhride, xxxi, xxxiv, 56, 100
Good, Starr, 26, 96
Gregory, Augusta, 1, 9, 48, 52, 67, 93, 99, 100, 102

Harrington, Christina, xxi, 91, 98
Heffernan, Thomas, xxiv
Hooke, Della, 27, 96

Illington, Ruth, xv, 33, 34, 39, 97, 98

Kildare, Co. Kildare, xiii, xvii, xxvii, xxix, xxxi, 9, 16, 20, 21, 26, 37, 38, 39, 53, 58, 69, 75, 74, 76, 77, 78, 81, 82, 83, 84, 85, 86, 87, 88, 89, 91, 92, 95, 97, 98, 100, 103, 104
Killare, Westmeath, xxxiii, 31, 36, 37, 38, 39
Kissane, Noel, 58, 91, 92, 95, 97, 100, 103
Knoppoge, Co. Kildare, 9, 10

Liscannor, Co. Clare, xxii, xxvii, xxix, 41, 42, 43, 44, 46, 47, 49
Logan, Patrick, 18, 95, 102
Lughnasa, 43

Mac Duagh, Colman, xiii, xxx
Mackey, James, 28, 96
MacMahon, Brian, 2, 93, 95
Macy, Gary, xxv, 54, 100
Maddox, Sylvia, 18, 95, 97
Mary of the Gael, xiii, 1, 4, 31, 73, 74, 87
Mel, bishop, xxv, xxvi, xxviii, 54, 81
Minehan, Rita, xv, 39, 78, 85, 88
Mullingar, Co. Westmeath, xv, 32, 33, 36, 97
Murray, Pius, xiii, xv, 44, 45, 99

Index

Newmarket-on-Fergus, Co. Clare, 42
Nugent, Louise, 25, 96

Ó Catháin, Séamas, 25, 53, 96, 100
O'Connell, Mary, 6, 92, 93, 94
O'Donoghue, Lawrence, 15
Ordo, 84, 85
Otherworld, xxii, 26, 31, 33, 43, 66, 72
Our Lady of Lourdes, 3, 8, 7, 9, 10, 45, 93

peacemaking, 31, 32, 34, 35, 39, 40, 51, 61
Penal Laws, 5, 18, 44, 47, 78, 86

Ray, Celeste, 4, 49, 50, 93, 99

Sheela-na-gig, 16, 17, 19, 20, 24, 25, 26, 78, 95, 96
Solas Bhríde, xv, 78, 85, 91, 98, 104
Soubirous, Bernadette, 3, 4, 93
syncretism, xxxi, 38, 44

Taylor, Lawrence, xxxiv, 4, 9, 93, 94

Uisneach, 31, 32, 36, 38
ultramontansim, xiv, 6, 97

Vita Prima, 31, 64, 104

well transformation, 29
Whelan, Dolores, xv, xxvii, xxx, 47, 61, 69, 70, 71, 72, 73, 92, 101, 102

www.ingramcontent.com/pod-product-compliance
Lightning Source LLC
Chambersburg PA
CBHW050554160426
43199CB00015B/2658